A POEM, A PLAY AND A SHORT STORY

ECHOES
of Emily

KATHERINE YANEZ-ARELLANO

www.trafford.com
North America & international
toll-free: 844-688-6899 (USA & Canada)
fax: 812 355 4082

CONTENTS

Fairies in the Attic

by Katherine Yanez-Arellano

Emily's mother had just brought down
a glittering magic-wand, a sparkling scalloped crown,
wings of gauze and gossamer, and a beaded gown
from a lofty antique trunk, a spirit's treasure trove.

"Fairies live in our attic!" I said, reaching for the ladder.
I could see the elfin creatures as real as any matter,
Through the portal up above, I could hear their impish laughter.
I could hear them faintly flutter on each enchanted rafter.

My sister tilted back her head, her eyelids at half-mask,
"It's just some ole costume: a stick, a cloth, some glass.
I don't wish to play with you. You're full of hallucinations."

"That's quite all right with me," I said. "How can you play?
You have no imagination."

Neither Moth nor Rust nor Family Intrigue

I was born in a museum. To the uninformed outsider, it was the palatial residence of the Williamsons of Candler, Georgia, furnished with mostly 18th century Georgian style antiques, reflecting tradition...stability...and...harmony. Assuring as these stately furnishings appeared, they belied the entangled, pernicious forces that beleaguered its inhabitants. One might find a more fitting metaphor in the Kudzu that entwined its stucco facade and invaded its latticed shuttered portals with all the intrigue of an Elizabethan drama. Its invasive vines protruded their way around the John Winthrop Singleton portrait of Mother.

The subject, donning a Prussian style fur hat and collar, was the epitome of sophistication down to her erudite expression and dismissive eyes. This prized portrait had been promised to me as a child, by the same-said mirror counterpart, as part of my inheritance. It was a foreboding maternal image. Not only was she displayed in a grotesquely ornate frame that cast gargoyle-like shadows over the ceiling but positioned under her was a bronze bust of a mythological Satyr. With his curved horns among his undulating locks, his chiseled cheeks, and his exaggerated grimace; the two of them, Mother and Satyr, appeared to be Machiavellian collaborators. One hand rocks the cradle; the other hand cradles rocks.

The year was 1950. My earliest memory began at the entrance way to the house. The foyer had large black and white Venetian marble tiles, great for playing hopscotch. I remember seeing my own image, a skinny-wisp of a child, in the ceiling-high, gold-gilded, baroque-framed mirror and listening to the ticking of the burnished-burlwood grandfather clock. The measured beat was echoed by the footsteps and the jingling of keys outside the front door. I remember I ran and gave Daddy a hug.

My first recollection of Mother, on the other hand, was quite different. Perceptions predate visual and auditorial memories. I knew better than to go near her. After Daddy embraced Mother in the foyer and gave her a kiss, he turned to me and said, "Give your mother a hug". I did so against my own better judgement. She pushed me away. I remember thinking she was Brunhilda though I'm sure, at the age of three, I had no word for Brunhilda, just the concept.

A couple of years later I was surprised when Gloria, my older sister by two years, said, "Mother is so beautiful". I thought at the time...is she talking about our mother?

"The Baby Jesus is beautiful", I said.

To the left of this foyer was the large formal dining room, the location of family gatherings for occasional festive meals when the air was permeated with the aroma of turkey and dressing, casseroles, fresh baked pecan pies, and ambrosia. We sat on white damask cushioned Chippendale chairs at a beautiful, eight-foot-long, mahogany Hepplewhite dining table draped in white linen. The table was set with Royal Crown Derby, peacock-designed, gold-rimmed china; long-stemmed, Waterford crystal goblets; and monogramed Gorham Chantilly sterling silverware.

The furnishings dictated Sunday attire. Gloria and I wore sashed and smocked dresses with full skirts girded with crinoline. Our feet dangled with shiny, black-patent-leather shoes over border-laced, white-nylon socks. Mother usually wore a stylish, monochrome silk or linen dress with small pumps. Daddy and my three brothers: Timmy, the eldest, born deaf and I suspect autistic (rather than compensating for his deafness, he avoided eye contact); Marc, my adopted brother, same age as my sister and raised as if they were twins (he and I were more twin-like by virtue of our shared sense of humor); and Leo, the bossiest (albeit the youngest); were appropriately dressed in coat and tie.

We appeared to be the idyllic family, well-mannered and pristine. We were encircled by megalithic, mahogany, Georgian breakfronts. At certain seasons of the year and with cosmic cooperation, a beam of sunlight would align through one of these austere china cabinets through the exquisite bubbles of its handblown glass to the delicate Wedgwood and Meissen within, revealing its fragile core.

Mother and I were separated at birth. The ambulance had gotten stuck in the driveway, so Mother gave birth to me at home without the benefit of anesthesia. Fortunately, Daddy was a doctor and was accustomed to bringing babies into the world. When the ambulance was unstuck, they took Mother to hospital; I was handed over to the nanny. The nanny's name, ironically, was the same name as my mother's name and mine. Our names were Emily. As a toddler, I must have over heard Emily, the nanny, referring to Emily, my mother, as Mrs. Williamson; because, I have been told, that I too called mother, Mrs. Williamson. Anything to overt confusion.

I also was told that, when I was a baby, Daddy, who was a general practitioner, had contracted tuberculosis from one of his patients and was recuperating in a sanitorium.

Thankfully he made a full recovery; but this meant he was not at home when I was a baby. Mother was left with a huge responsibility and a lot of stress when she already had a history of psychological problems.

Soon after Timmy was born and his deafness was discovered, Mother had been hospitalized for depression and had undergone shock treatments. Timmy was sent off to an out-of-state boarding school for the deaf. Gloria, born four years after Timmy, was the "perfect child". Somehow, Mother's self-esteem was wrapped up in Gloria's and Gloria's in hers. Instead of the estrangement of "baby-blues", the two of them formed an unusually strong, symbiotic attachment; an attachment that would cause Mother to escalate sibling rivalry to the point of family warfare.

It was Daddy's idea to adopt Marc and have a large family to hopefully ensure someone would be there to help Timmy in the high probability Timmy would outlive both his parents. Marc was added to the family as an infant in the same year Gloria was born. He and Gloria would later attend school together, often sharing the same teachers. They would have their own competitive issues. Gloria was the scholar; Marc was the personality.

In high school Marc befriended the teachers --- all the teachers, mine included, even to the point of cooking spaghetti dinners for some of them and doing odd jobs around their homes. On graduation day, while Gloria was scholastically recognized, Marc received so many awards: Good Citizenship, Most Likely to Succeed, etc., he had to have assistance in carrying them off the stage. Marc literally up-staged Gloria. I glanced over at Mother in the audience. She was sitting there with her arms crossed doing her Brunhilda impersonation.

I always got along great with Marc. Outgoing and funny, he provided much needed comic relief to an otherwise taciturn family. Gloria was a different story. I was told that, when I was born, Gloria had had a conniption fit. Unwittingly, I had added the fuel of jealousy to the fire of the terrible twos. It was a time of great wailing and gnashing of baby teeth… the beginning of our rivalry…who could bawl the loudest? I refer to this time as "Baby Bedlam" or the "Reign of Tears".

Gloria had nothing to cry about. Mother's loyalty to her would be unwavering as she masterfully wove Gloria's coat of many colors, carefully manipulating every warp and woof. Mother and I finally bonded on the understanding that Gloria was not to be dethroned. "You're the "sacrificial lamb", she said to me… and so the hierarchy was set. At first, I thought the unfairness was not Gloria's fault, but the fact that Gloria rarely played with me and would tell her friends not to play with me either, could not be denied.

Gloria was "the beauty" in the family. "Gloria is a classic beauty", Mother said. This fact was true, but it didn't hurt that she was allowed to have long braided hair adorned with bows. I scotch taped corn silks into my chopped off Buster Brown hairdo, but it didn't quite have the effect I was hoping for. In fact, it reminded me of my foiled attempt at playing hair stylist when I was six years old.

Both Gloria and I had received Madame Alexander dolls for Christmas: hers donning an embossed silk dress adorned with Belgium lace and golden ribbons; mine wearing a simple peasant blouse with a white cotton apron over a plain black felt skirt and matching vest. My doll's hair was parted in the middle and pulled back in a severe bun. It came with a styling comb. I didn't realize the doll's hair was glued down and was never meant to be disturbed. The more I combed it; the more frayed it became. Soon the doll took on the appearance of a scarecrow with straw sticking out in all directions. Upon witnessing the transfiguration of my doll, Gloria immediately put her Madame Alexander back in its box. She never touched or played with it again… neither did she thank me years later for helping her to increase her doll's value as a collector's item.

Gloria was "the brains" in the family. I inherited one of my sister's third-grade teachers, Mrs. Jameson. "You're not your sister, Gloria". Good eyesight, I thought.

Gloria was the type that would fret, "I know I flunked that exam!", only to discover she had made an A+. One time she was so wound up on report card day, she spun around like a top comparing her grades to the rest of ours. A short time after that, Mother told me to stop doing my homework.

Evidently, Mother wanted me to spend more time daydreaming. I overheard Mrs. Jameson tell Mother at a parent-teacher conference that daydreaming was what I excelled at, "She's sitting here, but she's someplace else". Apparently, you can be in two places at once.

Though physically at school, in my mind, I was in the kudzu jungle, a Gaudi-like undulating structure, sheltered by an organic canopy that was illumined by streams of sunlight breaking through its transparent leaves. It was a wilderness dripping with suspense and the promise of escape.

I discovered several footpaths amongst the large pines cloaked in leafy vines and headed in the direction of a large, look-out rock. I plowed through this labyrinth of fuzzy-leafed kudzu. I toddled over the jutting roots up to the top of this large, granite rock. Once there, I turned and surveyed my now diminutive home from a distance. Mother wasn't the center of my universe. God was showing me a different perspective.

Ironically, I had learned to use perspective in drawing by watching Daddy draw beautiful portraits of Gloria and studying Bronzini's "Portrait of a Young Scholar", one of many paintings which hung on our museum walls. By using various drawing techniques, I learned that one can turn a two-dimensional world into a three-dimensional one. Our eyes aren't really seeing reality. Looking at a railroad track between the long-connected rails, it appears that the rails converge at some point in the distance, but we know this isn't true. They run parallel. It's a trick of the eye. The artist can choose to mimic this illusion or adhere to the two-dimensional plane or use multiple perspectives.

Mrs. Jameson, in her need to say something positive to Mother, pointed to my drawing of a dancing snowman and said, "Emily really brought 'Frosty' to life."

I brought "Frosty" to life? And I thought it was "that old silk hat". Mrs. Jameson gave me an A in art.

This too aroused Gloria's ire. "No wonder she can draw; she draws all the time", Gloria quipped. This fact was true. Not doing my homework freed up a lot of my time.

To assuage Gloria's jealousy in the area of the arts, Gloria was given a violin. Occasionally she practiced, but eventually grew tired of it to everyone's relief. Mother didn't pressure her about the violin because, as I learned years later, her mother, Grandmother Kafka, had forced Mother as a child to perform on her violin in front of the Ladies Auxiliary. Mother had panicked and had run out of the room. She said her mother gave her the silent treatment for some time afterwards.

Generationally, the family suffered from the parental misconception that they, the parents, were in charge of their children's interest in life. God either puts music into their DNA or not. At the time Gloria was given violin lessons, Marc was given cello lessons. By contrast Marc loved to practice. I remember his solo recital of "It Came Upon the Midnight Clear" at the First

Baptist Church. While listening, Rev. Thornton had exuded an aura of serenity; his eyes closed, his hands calmly folded in his lap. Was he thinking of the lyrics, "Peace on the earth, good-will to men"? I glanced at Mother's inscrutable face. What was she thinking? Was that a smile or a grimace? Her arms were crossed and wound tighter than a latched-up Jump-in-the-Box. Was she pondering the opposing view… Jesus' own words in Matthew 10, "I came not to send peace, but a sword…And a man's foes shall be they of his own household"?

When my younger brother, Leo, came along, the rivalry between him and Marc was even more explosive. This rivalry, however, was of little interest to Mother and one in which she did not interfere other than to break up an occasional physical fight.

Marc had the advantage of being three years older than Leo. It was not by design but by necessity that Daddy leaned on Marc. Although Daddy had made a full recovery from tuberculosis, he was not in good general health. As a teenager, Marc cooked our breakfast, warmed up the car for Daddy, and helped to keep the household running before the servants arrived. In the summer Marc would drive Daddy around to visit his patients and thus a closer bond was formed between Marc and Daddy.

Leo was the baby-in-the-family… not the baby, spoiled and pampered… rather the baby at the end-of-the-line of exhausted parents. He also ended up being the baby-in-the-class. How Mother managed to get him registered for first grade when his birthday was late October, remains a mystery. The cutoff date was September first. Like a lot of boys, he was less mature than most of the girls his age, but because of the rush to have him leave-the-nest, he was also less mature than most of the boys. Not only does maturity count in the pecking order of boys, but maturity has a lot to do with readiness to read. Reading was a problem for Leo. I think too he may have had a speech impediment. Though Mother was a former schoolteacher, she employed the aid of Miss Henrietta, a passive spinstress who lived with her domineering mother (a role model I definitely didn't aspire to). Their house was between the school and our house. She was soft spoken and listened attentively to Leo reading out loud, which, not only helped with his reading, but also his verbal skills. She was a great help to Leo… and Mother. But it was no secret to his classmates that Leo stopped at Miss Henrietta's for tutoring.

The fact that Leo's math and science skills surpassed his language skills did little to undo the early labeling of being in the "yellow birds" reading group. I don't think Mother ever fully appreciated his left-brain aptitude. In high school he sailed through calculus, trigonometry, and breezed through chemistry classes…classes my right-brained Mother, I'm sure, avoided or tried to avoid when she was going through school.

Leo further felt ostracized from the family when as a five-year-old he had trouble memorizing his lines for a homemade movie Mother had scripted and Daddy filmed. Leo required a lot of patience. I remember trying to feed Leo his lines. Years later, it was Leo who corrected my memory. I thought I had played the part of the "Princess", but Leo said, "No, you were never the 'Princess'. You were the 'Wicked Stepsister'. Gloria was the 'Princess' and Marc was the 'Prince'". Leo told me he had been cut out of the film altogether.

While my fantasies protected my emerging ego, I don't know how Leo processed this superimposed narrative. I do recall, however, the day he played out his own attention-grabbing leading role and I was caught up in the drama.

It was late afternoon at home, the same day the Fire Marshal had presented his fire-safety program at Hartfield Avenue Elementary School. The Marshal went over the usual fire safety rules, most importantly, the don't-play-with-matches rule. Evidently, this served to ignite an idea in Leo's seven-year-old, combustible mind. He showed me a box of matches and told me to follow him downstairs. He set about piling up a small arsenal of wadded-up paper from his school notebook in the middle of the carpet. He struck a match and set the pile ablaze.

I couldn't move. The Kudzu vines poked in the window cracks and waved in the heat of the fire like Grandmother Williamson's copper angel chimes that spun in circles underneath the Christmas candles. These vines were pointing at the condemned. I could hear the crackling sound of Rev. Thornton's fist pounding on the pulpit admonishing the erring ones. The flames of hell edged their way closer and closer. The smell of the pernicious smoke piercing my nostrils on its inevitable rise to the upstairs.

"Wait 'til your father gets home", Mother's voice thundered, clearly not adhering to her own don't-be-a-tattletale rule. Mother quickly doused the flames thus saving us along with the luxurious antiques: the Queen Anne, the Chippendale, the Hepplewhite, the Steinway… expensive kindling… saved to ignite a family inferno another day.

It was one time I didn't look forward to the sound of Daddy's footsteps coming up all fifteen steps leading to the porch, the sound of his keys jingling, the sound of him opening the door, the sound of….

I'm someplace else. I'm Emily, Queen of the Kudzu Jungle, far, far away, swinging on my kudzu vine. Pow! Pow! Pow! I was rudely awakened. I screamed with each lashing of Daddy's leather belt. Leo said nothing. He took his punishment like a man. That day Leo was no longer the "baby" in the family. He became the "bully".

Sharks kill their siblings in the womb; humans bide their time. Looking back on my childhood to what I thought was engaging, imaginative play, was, in hindsight, orchestrated rehearsals for heart-piercing schemes and back-stabbing conspiracies that would tear the family apart. How innocently I participated in, and indeed took pleasure in, playing among the future spoils of war. Our opulent domicile, once a source of family pride, would someday become a source of division and plunder.

Little did I suspect one of the rare times my sister deigned to play with me was the foreshadowing of the treacherous tittle-tattle and rumormongering to come. Gloria and I were having a tea-party underneath the ebony grand piano in the living room. "Do-o-o-o tell, Miss Giddy Gaddy. I do implore you to share the latest tidbits of gossip", I would playfully say, mocking presumptuous sophisticates over a miniature willow-patterned teacup using the appropriate tilted pinky and the accompanying tilted voice.

Feigning the same, Gloria would respond, "Enchanted to do so, Miss Shakespeare Smith. Only to-o-o-o happy to indulge in delicious, backstabbing chitter-chatter. Oh, by-the-bye, do be a dearie and pass the lady fingers... so useful for stirring the pot".

By the same token, neither did it cross my mind that the exuberant, terrifying frenzy of playing "shoot'em up" with my brother, Leo, was a dress rehearsal for what was to come. "Bang! Bang! You're dead!", children playing with cap guns seemed innocuous fun under a sparkling crystal chandelier, but I would come to realize, the exhilaration of the game-of-chase would become horrifyingly real in the game of chase-the-inheritance orchestrated by Mother. In my naiveté, I enjoyed the hair-raising, heart-pounding excitement and put my assurance in the outward appearance of family stability. Completely trusting in what I thought were enduring bonds, I would confidently jump up onto the velveteen sofa expecting its firm foundation to catch me, flanked by the adjoining Queen Anne tables, underneath the all-knowing eyes of the Moroccan slave lamps.

Nor did the intoxicating dizziness of being swung around in the orbital path of the oriental carpet by my brother, Marc, prepare me for the reality of having my world spin-out-of-control by the break-up of our family. But there was one sibling that needed a family more than I.

"Why doesn't Timmy play?" I asked Mother, one time when he was home from Cochran School for the Deaf in upper-state Connecticut. She didn't answer. He had his own solitary activities, mainly watching movies. His favorite actors were men-of-few-words: Gary Cooper, Charles Bronson. But not only did he choose not to wear his hearing aid, he also didn't like looking people in the face which was a problem since he had to in order to read lips. He often wore a cap pulled down over his eyes and looked neither to the left nor to the right. He was polite, easy-going, and was totally oblivious to any competitive family fray. "Hear no evil; see no evil; speak no evil". Pardon the platitudes, but in Timmy's case, the shoe fit.

The museum turned into a dusty old mausoleum after the death of my father at age forty-five. I was fifteen at the time. Though fully recovered from tuberculosis, he had a weakened heart. He also had had one of his lungs removed being overly precautious; nevertheless, he wasn't cautious enough to stop smoking. The year was 1962, the year of my mourning. It was strangely juxtaposed to the ubiquitous image of Madalyn O'Hair, a bizarre mother figure, who, in a nightmare, handed me a coin with the motto, IN MOTHER WE TRUST.

We fell into poverty. Mother let go of the servants and no longer maintained the house nor the grounds; however, none of the antiques were sold. We lived on six thousand a year, despite the fact that Grandmother Kafka, who had moved in with us shortly after Daddy's death, was a millionaire. Grandmother was frugal to the extreme. "Don't run the vacuum cleaner. You'll wear it out".

The house was dusty and unkempt. Pollen blanketed the mahogany furniture giving it a yellow oche sheen. Kudzu vines protruded into vulnerable spaces reaching for the vintage wares. The air was stifling and difficult to breathe. I often suffered from asthma. Mother puffed away on her cigarettes.

Grandmother had experienced a failed cataract operation, possibly because of her high blood pressure. Although blind, she had a remarkable ability to make successful investments in the stock market and kept the complicated tabulations in her head. She had started investing from a two-hundred-fifty-dollar inheritance from her Aunt Clara. Aunt Clara, who had witnessed the bank-takeover of the farm, one of the largest in Iowa, after borrowing money to have the barn painted, carefully tucked her savings away under a rug. The financial gains of these carpet-sweepings turned blue-chip stocks went to Mother after Grandmother's death. Coupled with the antiques, these gains would form the fought-over inheritance.

Strange observation, Grandmother Kafka, who was very much a perfectionist (she was known to have had sewing bees at her home and later, after the ladies departed, would remove their stitches, and resew the quilts) never appeared to communicate much with Timmy. However, once she became handicapped herself, she always gave him a warm greeting. Nevertheless, it never occurred to her to educate, set up a trust, or help him out financially in any way. It was Daddy's side of the family that helped Timmy.

Daddy, as part of his internship, had moved Mother and Timmy, a newborn at the time, with him to a Native American reservation in Arizona. Due to the fact that Mother was immobilized by her depression (she didn't cook, clean, or tend to the baby), Daddy had to send for his sister, Aunt Isabell, to care for Timmy. She was his caregiver until they moved back to Georgia at which time Daddy hired a nanny to look after him. But sometimes, Timmy was Mother's responsibility.

When Timmy was around the age of five, he started walking a mile by himself over to Grandmother Williamson's house. Unfortunately, in that era, small towns were full of opinionated gossips. Mother was shunned by some of the ladies around town for being an absentee mother. To clarify that, Mother was always at home, we were the ones that had the run of the streets. Fortunately, in that era, small towns had remarkably safe streets.

I don't blame Timmy for going to Grandmother's house. She had her own goat and chickens. She used the fresh milk and eggs to make… Pineapple, Strawberry, Banana, Lemon-Orange, Carrot, and Chocolate cakes. Battered, baked, or caramelized… up-side-down or right-side-up… she always let us participate. We measured, packed, pounded, sprinkled, squeezed, graded, whipped according to her directions which were usually interspersed with Bible stories many of which had to do with sibling rivalry.

The one I took particular note of, was the one about a conniving mother, Rebecca, who, in cahoots with her favorite son, Jacob, instigated the "young goatskin" ruse in Genesis 27. Quite clever, indeed! I also noted that Jacob fled fearing retaliation from his brother, Esau, after usurping his birthright. Though later Jacob and Esau made their peace; ultimately, they went their separate ways. The trust was broken; the family was divided.

Unlike Rebecca, Grandmother Williamson had encouraged her children, now six adults, to get along with each other. And in turn, I and my siblings benefitted from their fidelity. We had the support of aunts, uncles, and cousins. Christmas time was particularly special when we gathered at Grandmother's beautifully decorated, Victorian-style home. We thrived around a family that maintained their ties into adulthood and understood the life-giving benefits of staying connected. It was a tradition I erroneously assumed would be continued by my immediate family.

One Christmas Timmy received a bicycle and his extended family taught him to ride it, so he had a better way of getting to Grandmother's house. When he grew into his teens and was old enough to drive, Grandmother gave him her 1949 Ford which he happily sported around town.

It was Daddy's sister, Aunt Victoria, who spent hours tutoring Timmy and paid for his training as a lab technician at a school in Buffalo, New York. At that time, it was the only program of its kind being taught to the deaf. She helped raise him and taught him the importance of showing up for work on time and always doing his best.

Strange coincidence, after leaving Georgia, Gloria's path would intersect with Timmy's in New York (God is often revealed in highly improbable circumstances to those who reflect). After being certified as a lab technician, Timmy obtained work in a medical laboratory in Buffalo. By chance, it was also the same location where Gloria was living. Gloria had met and married a New Yorker while they both were attending the University of Georgia. They and their four children were, at her husband's insistence, living in Buffalo a few miles away from Timmy. Naturally Timmy assumed he would be welcomed into her home. He showed up weekends and holidays, that is until… Gloria told him, in no uncertain terms, not to come over to the house anymore…not ever… never.

What was Timmy's egregious offense? It seems Timmy had made the faux pas of bringing a Christmas gift to the eldest child while forgetting to bring gifts to the other three, thus causing jealousy among Gloria's children. Gloria witnessed the contention that favoritism (though in Timmy's case, a matter of social ineptness rather than partiality) had bestowed on her own children. Ironically, she did not relate this to the contention that Mother's blatant favoritism had caused between herself and her own siblings. I wonder why? Hmmm…

Timmy's hospital position was low paying; but, to his credit, he proved a reliable employee. The family should be grateful he managed to independently support himself as long as he did. However, upon his retirement, it was learned his financial situation was not secure. He had a pitiful pension and had accumulated a lot of debt. After having a splenectomy his doctor advised him to move back to Georgia so his other family members could help look after him.

Once down south, he was promptly run off by Leo, too, "All he does is watch movies on television". This spoken by someone who, after Grandmother's death, swaggered around in a cowboy hat tilted forward, James-Dean-style … right out of the movie, "Giant", while propping his boots up on Mother's embossed Queen Anne coffee table.

I remember wondering to myself… who are these people? I inherited Timmy.

Mother played the siblings off of each other to justify her reputation as least-likely-to-be-nominated-Mother-of-the-Year and also to gain Gloria's sympathy to move her in with her to New York. Soon after she moved there, a will was drawn up. Gloria obtained power of attorney and placed Mother in a nursing home. I learned from Gloria that originally Marc, now stationed overseas with his wife and two children, was to be left out of the inheritance, presumably because he was adopted. After I objected, Marc was included, and I was left out. There was a conversation that Marc was more likely to sue than I, and according to Marc, when he visited Mother in New York, she suffered from dementia. I suffered from disillusionment. Timmy, Marc, and Leo were to receive token amounts. Gloria would receive all the antiques and the preponderance of the money.

After Mother's death, Leo, now married and living with his wife and four children in our hometown of Candler, made funeral arrangements for her to be interred in Georgia. At this juncture, all of us were married with the exception of Timmy. I traveled with my husband and son from our country home a couple of hours away. At the gravesite, the immediate family was seated in a row of cold medal, fold-out chairs underneath a forest green canopy advertising the Malaise Funeral Home. I was directed to the last chair on the end. After the service, Leo's pastor, not Rev. Thornton, started at the opposite end and shook each family member's hand, casting his eyes down reverently while nodding his head back-and-forth in the prescribed sympathetic manner, until he came to me. He abruptly did a one-hundred-eighty-degree pirouette and left without saying a word. Were these directions from Mother beyond the grave to further forsake her daughter? It was official. I had been publicly expelled from the family.

When my (family) forsake(s) me,

then the Lord will take me up. Psalm 27:10, KJV.

Years passed. The autumn Georgia sun cast dramatic shadows on to the chiseled marble and granite tombstones in the patina-tinted ancestral burial plot where Mother was buried. They reminded me of the gargoyle-like shadows cast by the John Winthrop Singleton portrait of Mother…the portrait that had been promised to me since childhood and had been given to Gloria. A storm cloud blew in from the north like a burial shroud covering the sky. The carefully delineated shadows disappeared. A light drizzle caused a nebulous steam to rise up from the slab. I heard a rumble. I pulled away some of the entrenched Kudzu vines clinging to Mother's headstone revealing the only resolution that I would ever receive this side of heaven. Etched on Mother's tombstone were the enigmatic words:

SOULS INTERTWINE WITH WHOM THEY MAY.

Katherine Yanez-Arellano

Murder At The Fitzwalter High School Reunion
BY KATHERINE YANEZ-ARELLANO

ACT I

INT. LADIES' LOCKERROOM OFF GYMNASIUM AT FITZGERALD HIGH – JUNE EVENING

36-year-old, petite female is sprawled out dead on floor under a row of sinks. She is dressed in a full skirted, knee-length, dusty-blue satin semiformal dress with a white corsage pinned to the left side of her scooped-necked bodice beneath her imitation pearl necklace. Next to her is an empty bottle of Wild Turkey. Miss. Thompson, a recently retired history teacher of Fitzwalter High and one of the organizers of the class of 1995's Reunion, is waiting to talk to Lieutenant Dan. Lt. Dan is busy on the phone with Sergeant Riley reporting the death of Emily Wilson, wife of alumnus, Chadwick Wilson. Lieutenant Dan Yeager is Miss Thompson's former pupil and one of the members of the Class of '95 along with his wife, Hazel, also an alumna. Hazel quietly observes as her husband takes charge of the situation.

LT. DAN:
(On phone to Sergeant Riley.) Sergeant Riley, come immediately to the Fitzwalter High Gym and secure all exits. Get forensics down here. There's a suspicious death. It could be a murder or just an accidental case of self-administered alcohol poisoning. (Turns off phone and turns attention to Miss. Thompson.)

MISS. THOMPSON:
I don't know …. I'm just so befuddled.

LT. DAN:
Yes, Miss. Thompson. This is quite a shock to us all. Please tell me exactly how you encountered the body.

MISS. THOMPSON:
I just came in here to powder my nose and there she was ... spread out on the floor with a bottle of Wild Turkey. Naturally, I thought she had just passed out drunk ... but, oh my, when I felt her wrist, she had no pulse.

LT. DAN:
And that's when you screamed?

MISS. THOMPSON
Yes, thank goodness you and Hazel are here at the reunion. This has been quite an ordeal. You remember being introduced to Emily Wilson, Chadwick's wife? (Hazel nods affirmatively.) Not from around here ... She spoke with a

heavy southern accent. You've probably seen her at previous reunions. I think Chadwick said she was from Candler. She had been seen earlier in the evening with Dave Richards, Sheila's ex, over by the punch bowl. Too much drinking, I'm afraid. Such a shame and an embarrassment to our favorite son, Chadwick. (Realizing her bias towards Chadwick is showing, quicky brags on Dan and his wife, Hazel.) And you Dan, we're so proud of you and your achievements. You were always so bright and analytical ... and your wife, Hazel, so imaginative and artistic. As they say, 'opposites attract'. (Hazel looks down demurely.)

LT. DAN:
Bright and analytical are accolades best left to describe our most herald alumnus, Chadwick Wilson.

MISS. THOMPSON:
I'm sure Chadwick had nothing to do with this unfortunate accident.

HAZEL:
Are you okay Miss. Thompson? Can I get you anything?

MISS. THOMPSON:
No, no thank you, Hazel. I'll be all right.

LT. DAN:
Whether a crime has been committed is up to Doc Cole and his autopsy report. If it proves to be foul play, as you know, husbands are always under suspicion. But even if it is ruled an accident, there will be a thorough inquiry starting immediately. Such awkward circumstances. The spirit of the reunion seems to be a glorification of Chadwick Wilson to a cult status ... whether a status of fame or a status of infamy, is yet to be determined.

MISS THOMPSON:
He was always such a sensitive boy. I'm sure he is devastated. Chadwick could have been anything he wanted to be. (Forgetting her bias again and speaking with florid gestures.) He was the brains and the brawn of the Class of '95. He comes from landed gentry - owners of a 200-acre pecan grove, as you well know. Everyone wanted a piece of Chadwick ... including our football coach. After his parents divorced, his grandmother raised him. Even though Coach campaigned relentlessly to have Chadwick play football, Granny Rutler never would allow it. Wrestling, yes ... football, no. Her son, Todd ...you remember Todd Rutler, big built like Chadwick? ... died while in training for the Ospreys ... head trauma. She devoted herself to Chadwick's mind. It was her ambition for him to obtain a business degree from a prestigious ivy league school. Thanks in part to her, he accomplished this and is now the pride of Fitzwalter. He comes from good stock.

LT. DAN:

I know all about the Rutlers. My grandfather was a sharecropper on their land. I used to help gather pecans in their grove when I was a boy. Chadwick and I grew up playing together.

MISS. THOMPSON:

Then you know he's not capable of murder.

LT. DAN:

I would find it hard to believe. No, the finality of murder would not appeal to Chadwick. He prefers a never-ending game of chess ... an ongoing mind-game ... the kill would only bring the fun to an end.

MISS. THOMPSON:

He wouldn't kill a flea ... Yes, he might taunt a flea. Remember the day he dangled that pesky, Ben Messer out the window by his feet? He could have dropped him on his head, but he didn't. I'll say one thing though, Ben Messer never said another disparaging word about Chadwick's mother.

LT. DAN:

As for that 200-acre farm, his now deceased grandfather bought up that land after the strike breaking of the railroad workers' union and becoming chief engineer ... a scab, a ruthless opportunist.

MISS. THOMPSON:

I was speaking more in terms of his grandmother.

LT. DAN:

One of my most vivid memories when I was visiting Chadwick was seeing a pair of scissors resting atop of the Bible. I looked inside and was shocked to see Granny Rutler's edited version, "Vengeance is mine, saith the ----. She had carefully cut out the Lord's name and any other jot or tittle she didn't agree with. Back in the day, a lot of people thought Granny had sought vengeance on Widow Brown. There was a suspicious fire at her house amongst rumors ole man Rutler had been keeping company there. They found charred pecan branches under the house. There were no pecan trees on Widow Brown's property. Couldn't prove anything though.

MISS. THOMPSON:

Conjecture and speculation.

LT. DAN:

I would say, if Chadwick learned a life lesson from the Rutlers, it was, 'You're the manipulator of your own fate'. By the way, whatever happened to Chadwick's big high school romance to Sheila? They were quite the 'IT' couple on campus.

MISS THOMPSON:

Speaking of manipulative, the little you-know-what was trying to derail Chadwick's chances at collegiate success. There was talk of marriage and Chadwick coming into the family's vending machine business. Thankfully, Granny would have none of it. She knew Chadwick was my Star Student and destined for the ivy leagues. Though that didn't stop Sheila from setting out her snares.

LT. DAN:

Specifically, what did Sheila do that you are aware of? I will be interrogating Sheila and all people of interest. You will admit, Miss. Thompson, young lovers are fraught with intense emotions.

MISS THOMPSON:

Emotions and connivances. Sheila did everything she could to hold Chadwick back. She temporarily broke up with him the night before his College Exams. He still received excellent scores ... highest in the class. She later claimed to be pregnant trying to trap him into marriage. Chadwick, though only 17, was ready to step-up-to-the-plate even over Granny's virulent objections. It turned out she wasn't pregnant, and they ended up going off to different colleges. Her father died soon after from a heart attack. She married Dave Richards, Chadwick's ole sparring partner. Chadwick and Dave were both on the Fitzwalter Wrestling Team. Ironic, right?

LT. DAN:

Right, ironic. I always wondered why Chadwick and Sheila didn't marry. So, Granny Rutler broke them up, um ....

MISS THOMPSON:

She nor I approved of Sheila's shenanigans. Today, Chadwick is a very successful entrepreneur, no thanks to her. He's into industrial chemicals, an international enterprise, you know.

LT. DAN:

So, I hear. Ok, Miss Thompson. Thank you for all your help. That will be all for now. Tell Sergeant Riley to meet me in the gym in a few minutes. Thanks. (Miss Thompson leaves and nods to Hazel who has been quietly listening.)

HAZEL:

So, essentially, Granny Rutler broke up Chadwick and Sheila.

LT. DAN:

Sheila married Dave on the rebound.

HAZEL:

So, it would seem. Rumor has it, Sheila wasn't too happy living in a trailer in her in-laws' backyard. She approached Chadwick with babe-in-arms while still married to Dave, begging him to take her back. Chadwick wasn't interested in raising Dave's progeny and he sent her packing. That wasn't enough to deter Sheila. She divorced husband numero uno and, according to Scuttlebutt Bertha, in a roundabout way, she's been after her golden boy ever since. With Bertha's promptings, among certain members of our class, their romance has taken on epic proportions. Romeo and Juliet could not have more ardent fans than Fitzwalter's own Star-Crossed-Lovers, Sheila and Charles.

LT. DAN:

If they were so much in love, why did they marry different people in the first place?

HAZEL:

Revenge marriage. I don't know. Distance and lack of communication. Something's not making sense.

CUT TO: INT. LOCATION: GYMNASIUM DECORATED FOR THE REUNION TIME: LATE EVENING

We see Lieutenant Dan pointing out directions for crowd control to Sergeant Riley. Members of the Class of '95 dressed in semi-formal attire are meandering around in a state of shock. They huddle into groups from their high school days. There is one independent exception, Hazel. She is unobtrusively listening to the conversations of people congregated around Bertha Quick, aka, Scuttlebutt Bertha, who is the honorary hub and gossip dispenser of the "in-crowd". Bertha is a strong, domineering woman.

BERTHA:

(Speaking in her naturally loud voice.) We all saw the way Chadwick's wife was dancing with Dave Richards when the band played the mambo. He always spikes the punch. Must have been giving her quite a few refills.

UNIDENTIFIED MALE IN CROWD #1:

Yea, a little bit of Sheila in my life, a little bit of Emily by my side.

BERTHA:

Hey, watch it. Don't be disrespectful of the dead. (Group snickering in muffled tones, their hands slightly covering their mouths.)

UNIDENTIFIED MALE IN CROWD #1

Oh! Excuse me. Are you referring to the lady that's stone-cold-dead?

UNIDENTIFIED MALE IN-CROWD #2

Well, I'm not talking about the one that's stone-cold-sober. (More muffled laughter.)

UNIDENTIFIED MALE IN-CROWD #3

She must have had a really ... stiff ... drink. (Loud laughter followed by shushing noises from same group.)

EXCHEERLEADER MARY JANE:

Hey, there's a soap opera for you. Maybe now, Sheila and Chadwick ... you know ... at long last ...

EXCHEERLEADER EVELYN:

Don't go there, girl. Don't even think it. Don't give the cops ideas. (Girls sigh with simpering romantic expressions on their faces.)

LT. DAN:

(Points to the coach's office and talks to Sergeant Riley.) Secure all doors and set up a make-shift interrogation room in the coach's office. We'll start with Chadwick Wilson and then his former high school sweetheart, Sheila Blake.

SERGEANT RILEY:

Some of the people are saying they have to call home to their babysitters.

LT. DAN:

Let them call and make arrangements. This looks like an all-nighter. Nobody leaves 'til I say so.

CUT TO: INT. LOCATION: GYM OFFICE/MAKE-SHIFT INTERROGATION ROOM TIME: NIGHT

We see Lieutenant Dan taking notes as he interrogates Chadwick Wilson. Both are seated. Chadwick makes sobbing noises. No tears are detected by Lt. Dan as he scrutinizes Chadwick's face. Lt. Dan hands him a tissue anyway. Chadwick folds it into a neat, small rectangle and dabs the corners of his eyes and then puts it in his pocket.

LT. DAN:

It's been a sad reunion, Chadwick. Sorry about your wife, Emily. This is a very difficult time for you, I'm sure. You understand these are standard questions ... nothing personal. Our trivial boyhood scraps are way past bygones.

CHADWICK:

(Chadwick composes himself.) No, we haven't been in an adversarial stance since that playground scuffle in the third grade. We were both sent to Principal Newton's office.

LT. DAN:

Oh, I remember it clearly, I had you penned to the ground 'til you threw dirt in my eyes.

CHADWICK:

Get them when they're down, I always say. Just kidding, as I recall, Newton sympathized with me when I told him you started the fight to prove you could take down the biggest kid in the class. He let me go back to my room while he called your parents. (Chadwick shakes head with a slight grin then seemingly remembers the present situation and looks pleadingly.) But hey, we became best friends after that, best buddies. I need you, pal. I can't believe this is happening. (Puts hands over face and moans.)

LT. DAN:

(Leans forward and sympathetically nods head. Takes notes.) So, tell me about your wife, Emily. She's not from around here. Exactly when and where did you two meet?

CHADWICK:

We met at the Barkley Arms in Atlanta back when I was doing real estate in 2000. She was teaching school.

LT. DAN:

Barkley Arms? A bar?

CHADWICK:

An apartment club house, one of the amenities ... a social meeting place that happened to sell libations.

LT. DAN:

Was Emily known for drinking to excess? Was she accustomed to alcohol? Addicted? Alcohol ... in her family's background?

CHADWICK:

No, as a matter of fact, she rarely drank at all. Strange, this is so unlike her. I saw her and Dave Richards over at the punch bowl. He always was a smooth talker with the ladies. Reputation as a boozer too. Everyone here saw him dancing with Emily. In fact, everyone else stopped dancing and formed a circle around them.

LT. DAN:

Why weren't you dancing with your wife?

CHADWICK:

Corns ... corns and bunions.

LT. DAN:

(Straightens up in his seat. Rolls his eyes. Continues taking notes.) Dave used to be a close friend of yours back in high school ... sparing partners on the wrestling team ... a pretty competitive relationship developed between you two. Later, he married your high school sweetheart, Sheila, and now he's seen dancing with your wife, Emily. That would make some men jealous. Wouldn't you say?

CHADWICK:

I gave him permission. Actually, Emily and I have been separated for some time. I sleep at the office. We're staying married until our son graduates high school.

LT. DAN:

Interesting, maybe you wanted them to be seen dancing together to send some sort of message. (Lt. Dan stares questioningly into Chadwick's eyes.) You and Shelia were quite an item back in the day. People were surprised when Shelia upped-and-married Dave, instead of you.

CHADWICK:

Ancient history. We parted ways after high school. As far as the reunion goes, I was just circulating and catching-up with my classmates and teachers. Miss. Thompson's the greatest. I've maintained strong connections with her and some of my classmates over the years. I wasn't keeping tabs on Emily or Sheila.

LT. DAN:

You're living in Carroll County presently, correct? (Chadwick nods affirmatively.) Yes, you need to give us a list of any and all close ties you've maintained here and also your business associates' names and phone numbers from Carroll County. That will be all for now. Leave all the required information with Sargent Riley outside this office. (Chadwick leaves.)

LT. DAN: (CONT.)

(Turns to Sergeant Riley who is at door.) Bring in Sheila Blake.

SERGEANT RILEY:

That would be Sheila Turner now, Sir.

LT. DAN:

Then bring in Sheila Turner. Am I supposed to keep up with her multiple marriages?

SERGEANT RILEY:

She's on her third marriage. Married shortly after the last reunion.

LT. DAN:

Fill me in.

SERGEANT RILEY:

Ronny Blake, her second husband. Married after the first reunion in 2000. Died of self-inflicted asphyxiation. You remember Ronny, the only child of Claire and Frederick Blake. A shame he came down with some kind of incurable illness right after he inherited his parents' estate. The town was aware of his illness when Sheila consented to marrying him. The suicide was a shock. She rebounded by marrying Johnathan Turner, coincidently, another member of the Fitzwalter class of '95, right after the second reunion in 2005.

LT. DAN:

I know who Johnathan Turner is. Say wasn't he, for real, headed for the NFL?

SERGEANT RILEY:

Never made it ... busted kneecap finished off his career.

LT. DAN:

Guess Granny Rutler was right about all your eggs ... so forth and so on. Send her in. (LT. Dan notes a knowing glance exchanged between Chadwick and Sheila as they pass each other at the office entrance where Chadwick is filling out forms.)

LT. DAN: CONT.

Have a seat Ms. Turner, now, is it? (A statuesque, attractive brunette enters room. Slight questioning tilt in Lt. Dan's voice as he pronounces Turner.)

SHEILA:

(Nods.) Thank you, Daniel. (Exaggerated emphasis on his given name. Beguilingly stares into Dan's eyes.) I haven't seen much of you and your wife lately. How is Hazel? I didn't see her tonight. Is she at the reunion?

LT. DAN:

(Loosens his tie and lowers his voice an octave.) No one's called me Daniel since my mother passed. (Sheepishly cast eyes down then regains composure and clears throat.) Yes, Hazel's here ... just shy, you know. So where were you in the gym area in relation to the deceased around 11:30-11:45 when Miss Thompson discovered the body?

SHEILA:

Why Daniel, I was going over some old cheers with Mary Jane and Evelyn. You remember, "The FHS Foxes stick together; FHS, a pack forever".

LT. DAN:

Yes, you were a part of a very close-knit clique between certain members of the class. I'd say mostly cheerleaders and jocks and a few exceptions like Bertha

Quick, who is presently working in the cafeteria here at the school. You realize she's been going around for years being the "Gossip Queen" of the "in-crowd".

SHEILA:

Oh, Scuttlebutt's harmless. She's abuzz with news. It's her opinion my ex, Dave Richards, has something to do with this intoxication incident. I wouldn't doubt it. They did say this was alcohol related, didn't they? I'd put him down in your little notebook.

LT. DAN:

Thank you for your suggestion. That will be all for now. Don't leave the area. (Sheila leaves the room and Lt. Dan calls out the door.) Sergeant Riley.

LT. DAN: CONT.

(Sergeant Riley sticks his head in at the door.) Get me all the videos and photographs taken at the reunion including the arrival and the earlier luncheon in the day. And send in Dave Richards, Sergeant.

SERGEANT RILEY:

He appears to be intoxicated, Sir.

LT. DAN:

Well, carry him in. I need to evaluate his state of competency.

SERGEANT RILEY:

Right away, Sir. (We see Dave Richards, an athletic-built man, stagger in on the arm of Sergeant Riley. Sergeant Riley holds him up in the interrogation chair.)

LT. DAN:

(Speaks in slightly elevated, patronizing voice.) Dave .... Dave ... this is Dan, your ole classmate, Dan Yeager.

DAVE:

(Speaks in intoxicated slur.) Dan? ... Lieutenant Dan, my ole pal, Dan. How's it going? Say what? I'm doing fine. Great reunion. See my ole friends, my ex-wife. Great punch by-the-way ... lots of pretty ladies.

LT. DAN:

Yes, your ex ... Sheila is here. Are you all on speaking terms?

DAVE:

(Slurs speech.) That witch? Th-inks she's still prom queen. Have to ... get along ... the kid, you know. I'm still livin' in the trailer ... back of Mom and Dad's house ... landscaping business. Never g-o-o-o-d enough for the "Princes". How's your wife, Hazel? You know, Hazel's always been a "good girl". Quiet ... in-her-own-world ... never ran with "the clique".

LT. DAN:

Neither of us qualified for the "in-crowd". She is doing fine. Thanks for asking. Where were you in relationship with Emily Wilson earlier this evening?

DAVE:

Emily who, ... what, when, where...why?

LT. DAN:

Exactly. You were seen dancing with Emily shortly before her death.

DAVE:

(Sits up on his own. Begins to talk in a normal voice.) Death? Who are you talking about? Emily who? Oh, Wilson. Chadwick's wife? No, no, I remember dancing with her. Everybody goaded me into it.

LT. DAN:

Goaded you into it? Who egged you on, specifically?

DAVE:

I don't know. Bertha for one. You know, her hanger-on-errs, Mary Jane, Evelyn, ... a bunch of them. Deceased? What's going on here?

LT. DAN:

Emily Wilson was found dead in the ladies' locker room at 11:45, apparently from an alcohol overdose. What do you know about Emily?

DAVE:

Nothing. I just know she's Chadwick's wife. We talked a little. She's not from around here. What is this? I just danced with her ... what's the big deal?

LT. DAN:

OK, don't leave Fitzwalter.

DAVE:

Is this a murder case? Am I a suspect?

LT. DAN:

We've yet to determine the cause of death. We'll know more after we get the autopsy results. Will keep you informed. Appreciate your cooperation, Dave. Someone will drive you home. (Dave leaves room.)

LT.DAN: CONT.

(Turns to Sergeant Riley.) Have one of my officers drive Dave home and tell everyone else they are free to leave. Take the bottle of Wild Turkey and all trash bags in the area for evidence. Secure all entrances and leave a patrolman on duty.

SERGEANT RILEY:

Right, Sir. This is one for the Yearbook.

LT. DAN:

I hear you. Tell Hazel to bring the car around. It's been a long night.

SERGEANT RILEY:

It's morning now, Sir. See you at Headquarters shortly.

LT. DAN:

Get some shuteye, Serge. See you around 10.

SERGEANT RILEY:

Thanks.

CUT TO: INT. LOCATION: DAN AND HAZEL'S KITCHEN.
TIME: LATE MORNING FOLLOWING THE REUNION

We see Lieutenant Dan and wife, Hazel having breakfast in their modest kitchen/dining area. Lt. Dan's head is buried in a newspaper, but occasionally looks up to acknowledge Hazel. Hazel appears contemplative.

HAZEL:

Something dawned on me.

LT. DAN:

Something is always dawning on you. You and the sun ... every day another dawning. Pass the marmalade. Apple? ... why didn't it dawn on you to get orange marmalade? You know it's my favorite.

HAZEL:

Apples and oranges ... that's exactly what I'm talking about. Sheila Blake and Sheila Turner. Don't you get it? ... what's the difference?

LT. DAN:

Where's my coffee?

HAZEL:

Every class reunion ... Bertha has a new scoop of gossip, a new flavor. All centered around the great question ... who will be Sheila's next alumnus husband? Every five years, around the time of the reunion, Sheila gets a divorce or becomes a widow and marries soon after ... always another former classmate ... always a former friend of Chadwick's. Don't you see the pattern?

LT. DAN:

I get that I need a cup of coffee. Hey, Popcorn Brain, I mean Honey Bun. I can't follow this. I've got to get the coroner's report. Bye, Sweetheart. (Hazel gives Dan her cup of coffee. He kisses Hazel as she stares out the window in deep thought. Dan hurriedly finishes coffee, grabs his briefcase, and leaves.)

HAZEL:

(Talking to herself.) Odd, very odd ... It's like a spouse hunting expedition every five years ... Sheila actually sees the reunion as a matchmaking event. But who is the Matchmaker?

CUT TO: INT. LOCATION: Coroner's morgue.
Time: Midday

We see Lt. Dan and Doc Cole in the autopsy room with Emily's body under a sheet on a table.

LT. DAN:

What 'cha got for me Doc? Alcohol poisoning, no doubt ... too much Wild Turkey?

DOC COLE:

Well, it's wild something. Look at this. (Dr. Cole lifts sheet covering Emily's corpse showing the area just below the clavicle.)

LT. DAN:

She looks like she has some kind of a rash on her left side.

DOC COLE:

Dermatitis in the thoracic outlet, the space between the clavicle and her first rib on her left ventricle, exactly where her corsage was pinned.

LT. DAN:

So, she was allergic to flowers. A lot of people are allergic to flowers. That doesn't prove a crime. Besides, all the ladies were wearing corsages at the reunion.

DOC COLE:

Corsages ... yes, but not the same. I called around the local florist to find the one responsible for the event's corsages.

LT. DAN:

What did you find out?

DOC COLE:

The owner of Main Street Florist said she provided the nosegays. She showed me a sample. They were composed of white freesia, a small funnel-shaped flower with long narrow leaves very similar in appearance to oleander.

LT. DAN:

Nerium oleander, an ornamental-shrub every part of which is deadly: flowers, stems, leaves. It blossoms profusely and is found in abundance in this area.

DOC COLE:

The flowers of the oleander are slightly different from the freesia ... they have five petals instead of the six that are characteristic of the freesia. That was the give-away, a subtle difference ... not likely to be noticed during the festivities. The corsage found on the victim is made up of oleander, not freesia. And if you look closely in the center of her dermatitis, there is a pronounced swollen lesion in close proximity to where one might expect to see a pinprick from a corsage ... right over her heart.

LT. DAN:

What are we talking here, a purloined corsage? Oleander ... Some consider it the most poisonous plant on earth. Right up there with belladonna and hemlock.

DOC COLE:

Exactly, Nerium oleander contains cardiac glycosides that can cause cardiac arrhythmias. The oleander was not ingested but was introduced to the bloodstream through a pinprick. Certainly, when combined with alcohol, the two in conjunction would be lethal.

LT. DAN:

We're definitely dealing with a homicide, then. We're officially calling it a poisoning. But for now, don't say anything to the press about the type of poison or how it was administered.

DOC COLE:

I'll keep it close to my vest.

LT. DAN:

Oh, please ... I'll take the corsage in as evidence.

DOC COLE:

Don't allow anyone to incinerate the body. Even breathing smoke from burning oleander has been known to be toxic. Besides, we don't want to destroy the evidence.

LT. DAN:

I'll tell forensics to take precautions. Thanks Doc.

ACT II

CUT TO: EXT. LOCATION: Outside Fitzwalter High TIME: Late morning

We see ATLANTA ON-THE-SPOT NEWS van and camera crew and Miss. Thompson along with curiosity seekers in front of Fitzwalter High School. Reporter Andy Flint is questioning Miss. Thompson. The tv, visible inside the van, shows a picture of Emily Wilson on her wedding day with husband, Chadwick Wilson. Camera takes close-up of Andy Flint giving a televised interview to Miss. Thompson in front of school.

ANDY FLINT:

(Facing camera.) Hi! I'm Andy Flint reporting today from Fitzwalter, Georgia for the Atlanta On-The-Spot News. We are here at Fitzwalter High School, the scene of a tragic homicide at a class reunion.

MISS THOMPSON:

(Miss Thompson is shaking her head.) Unbelievable. Unbelievable.

ANDY FLINT:

Last Saturday night, around 11:45 PM. Miss. Thompson, a retired history teacher here at Fitzwalter High, made the gruesome discovery of the body of Emilia Louise Wilson. Ms. Wilson was an attendee of the 1995 class reunion with her husband Chadwick Wilson, an honored alumnus. Earlier that same day, Mr. Wilson had been recognized as the Most-Successful-Graduate of the Class of '95. What a sad turn of events as his wife's body was discovered in the ladies' locker room. The whole class is in a state of shock. It appeared initially that Mrs. Wilson died of an overdose of alcohol; however, on further investigation, the alcohol was found to be a catalyst for another toxin. The release of the name of that poison is pending further confirmation by the Georgia Poison Center. No motive has been established.

ANDY FLINT: CONT.

(Turns his attention to Miss Thompson for the-on-camera-interview.) Exactly where did you find the body of Emily Wilson and what were the circumstances?

MISS. THOMPSON:

My stars, I couldn't believe it. I thought Ms. Wilson had consumed too much Wild Turkey. There was a bottle of it lying next to her in the ladies' locker room.

It's such a shock to now hear her death has been pronounced a homicide. That sort of thing just doesn't happen here in our peaceful town of Fitzwalter.

ANDY FLINT:

Fitzwalter, a typical small town in southern Georgia. You're the historian, Miss Thompson. Give us some background on Fitzwalter.

MISS THOMPSON:

Well, not exactly typical. You might say Fitzwalter is exceptional, an unlikely amalgamation. Founded in 1868 by the venerable Philias P. Fitzwalter, a hallowed Civil War veteran ... might I add, from the Union side. The War was over. He and others were eager to put it behind them. He had had enough of cold northern winters and desired to make his home in the warmer climate of Georgia. He had been charmed by one of the local southern belles. Married her and campaigned for other northern veterans to move to the warm south too. A few hundred northern veterans joined him in creating a town dedicated to the peaceful coexistence of northerners and southerners alike.

ANDY FLINT:

So, what you're saying is that many of the townsfolk that are living here today are descendants of Yankee carpetbaggers and scallywags. (Looks into the camera with a big grin on his face.) Just joking. No offense folks. No letters, please.

MISS. THOMPSON:

Those are rather derogatory terms, Mr. Flint. We refer to our honorable ancestors as men with the foresight to seek opportunities that were both advantageous to their contrite brothers-in-arms, as well as to themselves. It's a town of peaceful reconciliation.

ANDY FLINT:

Right. And briefly, Miss Thompson, would you say that the victim, Emily Wilson, was a daughter of Fitzwalter.

MISS. THOMPSON:

Oh, dearie me, no. She's originally from the outskirts of Atlanta ... Candler, I believe.

ANDY FLINT:

An outsider. Okay. Thank you very much for your perspective, Miss. Thompson. (Miss. Thompson steps away and Andy Flint turns and faces the camera directly.) We will be following this story as it develops and now a word from Jerry at traffic patrol. Take it away Jer.

CUT TO: INT. LOCATION: Fiztwalter Police Headquarters, Lt. Dan's office
TIME: Late morning.

We see Sergeant Riley announce the entrance of Katrina Sommers to Lt. Dan. Riley leaves during the interview but reenters as Sommers is leaving.

SERGEANT RILEY:
A visitor, Sir. A young lady from Atlanta, a Ms. Katrina Sommers. Said she heard about the murder of Ms. Wilson, on the 11 o'clock news. She was a close friend of the deceased and said she might have some relevant information concerning the case.

LT. DAN:
Bring her in, Serge. (Stands up as Katrina Sommers, a thirtyish distraught-looking woman, enters the room. Sergeant Riley leaves.) Please have a seat, Ms. Sommers. his desk.) What can I do for you?

KATRINA:
(Katrina's eyes are red and puffy.) Please call me Katrina. (Gets out a photo from her purse showing a younger Emily Wilson and herself smiling together in what appears to be a college dorm room. Hands it to Lt. Dan.) I'm just devastated by Emilia's murder. I've been driving for hours hoping to talk to someone about the case. See, Emilia was my dearest and best friend. (Her voice cracks from emotion as tears well up in her eyes. (Lt. Dan gives her a tissue. She wipes tears from her cheeks.) Give me a moment.

LT. DAN:
Take your time. I understand. (Short pause.) So, how long have you known Emilia or Emily, Katrina? I take it you were roommates in college from this photo.

KATRINA:
I knew Emily when she was Emilia. Yes, we met at college. We've been close ever since. It was her husband's idea to call her Emily. He read somewhere in one of his many "Confidence" books that one can more easily influence people if one doesn't use an off-putting formal name. I never knew Chad as Chadwick.

LT. DAN:
Interesting. What more can you tell us about ... Chad ... and about their relationship.

KATRINA:
If Chad was a big success, you'd never know it by that hovel of a house they lived in.

LT. DAN:

I'm looking at a photo of their residence on the computer now. Please continue.

KATRINA:

Business calls were routed to the house. Emilia helped him with the business ... answering the phone, taking orders ... that sort of thing. Never allowed her to handle the business books though. Strange since she was in charge of paying household bills ... from a very paltry allowance, I might add.

LT. DAN:

Tight with the money, would you say?

KATRINA:

Imagine, a Harvard graduate keeping his wife in poverty. Whether he really has any money, who knows? I do believe he was struggling when they first met. He was in real estate and the bottom had just dropped out of the market. He was driving around in an old Citroen, a foreign car. Had a fancy hydropneumatics suspension system that could elevate the car if you were driving over rough terrain. But unfortunately, it needed repairs, and he was too broke to get it fixed. The Citroen died right after they married ... Good timing for him. Emilia had a paid-for Maverick only a few years old.

LT. DAN:

I'm sure foreign parts are quite expensive.

KATRINA:

On their honeymoon, they drove down to Florida in the Maverick and stayed with his mother who was living there at the time. Emilia related a conversation to me that went on between Chad and his mother. On discovering Emilia was a schoolteacher, his mother said, right in front of her, 'I'm surprised you didn't marry someone with more potential'.

LT. DAN:

In other words, more money?

KATRINA:

As soon as they returned from Florida, he promptly traded in her Maverick for an older van which made no sense. Whatever little savings she had in her name, she soon had no more. 'I follow the golden rule ... He who has the gold, rules,' was his favorite saying.

LT. DAN:

What was her attitude about Chad starting his own business?

KATRINA:

Emilia was always one-hundred-percent supportive of Chad's endeavors and encouraged his entrepreneurship. But it was ridiculous that he wouldn't even buy curtains for their house or a stick of new furniture. All they had were a few remnants from his college days.

LT. DAN:

His former teacher, Miss Thompson, and indeed his whole class are under the impression that he is the owner of a very successful international chemical company.

KATRINA:

Who knows the truth?

LT. DAN:

That's what we're trying to discover ... the truth. Did he talk much about his business?

KATRINA:

He was always trying to get my husband to invest in it. We didn't have any money to invest. We thought he was full of pipe dreams anyway.

LT. DAN:

But he stayed in business. He never filed for bankruptcy.

KATRINA:

True. Curious that he always poor-mouthed. When her mother gave her money to buy curtains, he would come up with an excuse to take the money ... 'Business is slow this month and I need it to pay my employees'. He pulled that stunt several times. I remember her mother finally bought her curtains for the sake of decency. Her mother saw him for the thief that he was, but she got the best of him some years later.

LT. DAN:

Oh, how was that?

KATRINA:

Chad had devised a plan to leave Emilia and he thought he'd be off-the-hook for having to supply her with a house in the divorce. He figured if he spent money renovating his mother-in-law's house, he could send his wife back to her, claiming by way of investment, he had fulfilled his obligation. Little did he suspect that after the renovations were done, her mother would sue him for unauthorized work.

LT. DAN:

Why didn't Emilia leave at that point?

KATRINA:

She didn't have the whole picture. She suffered from divided-fidelity and had to go to the ER for stress. Ironically the bill from the ER caused her more stress. She had no understanding of the hostility between her husband and her mother. They had instantly disliked each other; he referring to her as a "cultured bum", and she referring to him as "nouveau intelligentsia".

LT. DAN:

Chadwick didn't have good role-models.

KATRINA:

His family was in a culture of divorce. According to Emilia, divorce was traditionally encouraged by the good-ole-brothers in the family. Their wives sin? ... reacting to their husbands' growing aloofness. The husbands of course would try to figure out a way to curtail their legal financial responsibilities. One brother, a real estate tycoon who had divorced multiple times, purchased a motel, and put three of his exes in it together. The judge said it fulfilled his legal obligation.

LT. DAN:

Sounds like he was trying a similar ploy to get off-the-hook ... by remodeling his mother-in-law's house. Do you have anymore insightful stories?

KATRINA:

Chad never had an original idea of his own. Emelia remembers Chad asking his mother a very-telling question early on in the marriage. 'Mother, you remember Uncle Joe whose wife divorced him ... What was the reason for the divorce?'. His mother said it was because her brother thought the money, he earned, was his money alone. He spent it on motorbikes and boats ... toys for himself instead of their home. A lightbulb must have gone off in Chad's head.

LT. DAN:

But you said, he never spent his money on the trimmings of success. He did the opposite. According to you, when they married, they had a respectable car and he traded it in for a ... hey, in fact, the couple drove down to the reunion in an old, broken-down, smoke-bellowing van. I was wondering how it ever passed an emissions inspection.

KATRINA:

Chad was too clever to have anything of value out in the open that could be claimed in a divorce. He did indulge himself in a classic old car once, a 1959 Cadillac Eldorado. I think it became clear to him that Emilia was never going to divorce him over money issues. She never complained about the fact that she lived, literally, in a shotgun house out in the middle of nowhere. I say 'she' because he was traveling during the week and was seldom at home.

LT. DAN:

So, what was the central problem in the marriage? Infidelity? I went to Fitzwalter High with Chadwick. At the time, he was going with one of the cheerleaders named Sheila. They were a pretty serious couple. Everyone expected them to get married. Did Emily, Emilia that is, ever mention someone named Sheila?

KATRINA:

Not to me.

LT. DAN:

Emilia never thought anything about his constant traveling?

KATRINIA:

Interesting you should ask that. Emilia told me one time that Chad said, 'No man leaves a woman, unless he has another to go to'. She blew it off, feeling a false sense of security. They had just had a son and, as he said, 'He's your ace-in-the hole'. But in hindsight it seems he was trying to run her off, right about the time he bought his first computer. And I mean literally ... run her off or have her run off.

LT. DAN:

Run her off?

KATRINA:

He bought the Cadillac in Florida from his aunt. His aunt had kept it in good condition. While he drove it back to Georgia with their young son in the car along Interstate 95, he had Emilia follow behind in the old van. Suddenly, he sped ahead out of sight. It was all she could do to catch up with him in that old rickety van. She finally did and motioned him off the road. She told him, in no-uncertain-terms, he was to keep the van insight in his rearview mirror at all times. It wasn't long after that, that a scruffy-looking man driving a beat up car, side-swiped her van running her off the road. Chad saw the attempted hijacking in his review mirror and confronted the guy. It was a holiday and there were no patrolmen in sight. After waiting over an hour, they got tired and let him go. Not only did Chad's hands appear clean; he came out the hero.

LT. DAN:

That sounds like Chadwick. But there's no history of physical violence. We checked.

KATRINA:

Like I said, his hands were always clean. He just seemed to put her in danger, making someone else the bad guy.

LT. DAN:

Was there a pattern of him manipulating a situation that would possibly show malicious intent?

KATRINA:

There was another time when he was less-than-attentive after Emilia had had surgery. She was having complications which led to a profuse nosebleed. After delaying her pleas for help, he finally took her to hospital.

LT. DAN:

Their son was there?

KATRINA:

Yes, he witnessed it. All the way to the hospital, while her nose was bleeding, Chad was screaming and yelling at her ... making her bleed ten times worse. So, when they arrived, she told the attendants, 'Get that man away from me'. Well, you can imagine what they thought. They called the police. Chad was interrogated for wife-beating for over an hour while Emilia was lying on a gurney essentially being ignored. With all the drama, the bleeding was so exasperated, she almost died. She obviously recouped, but sometime later, she overheard him bragging over the phone to one of his good-ole-boys, 'A husband can emotionally abuse his wife and the law can't do a thing about it'.

LT. DAN:

Throw dirt in their eyes when they're down ... could be his M.O., but none of this rises to the level of premeditation. Taking advantage of a situation cannot be directly linked to murder, though it can certainly make one suspicious.

KATRINA:

Right.

LT. DAN:

Right.

KATRINA:

In other words, he could double, triple the amount of weed killer in a vegetable garden that she was primarily eating from, and get off scot-free, as long as he didn't directly put weedkiller in her food.

LT. DAN:

Devious ... but not criminal. Thank you for making the trip. You've been very helpful. Let me know if you think of anything else. We'll be in touch. (Stands while Katrina leaves room. Sergeant Riley enters.)

KATRINA:

But like you say, 'It does make one suspicious'. Thank you, Lieutenant. (She passes by Sergeant Riley entering.) Good day.

SERGEANT RILEY:

Good day. (Tips hat at Katrina and turns toward Lt. Dan with a questioning look on his face.) What's up?

LT. DAN:

(Points out copy of the wedding photo of the Wilsons' marriage shown on the 11 o'clock news.) What do you see here, Serge?

SERGEANT RILEY:

(Carefully looks at photo.) Hey, that's the lady that just left. Looks like she was the maid-of-honor.

LT. DAN:

Katrina Sommers. What else stands out?

SERGEANT RILEY:

Small wedding ... I see the couple, the preacher, Katrina Sommers, and a lady identified as Emily's aunt. No other family members or friends in attendance. Official looking, I'd say, rather than celebratory. Emily's wearing a wedding band; he's not. There's no engagement ring.

LT. DAN:

What else? (Riley shakes his head.)

LT. DAN: (CONT.)

The dress, the dress. It's the same dress she was wearing at the reunion ... minus the corsage.

SERGEANT RILEY:

You're right. What does that mean?

LT. DAN:

Maybe Chadwick's not the big success the people back home think he is. Let's check out pictures from past reunions for the class of '95. (Lt. Dan searches his computer. Sergeant Riley looks over his shoulder.) The first, second, third reunion pictures ... all the same dress.

SERGEANT RILEY:

What, the man can't afford a new dress for his wife at his own honored reunion?

LT. DAN:

Maybe she was threatening to tell the true facts about Fitzwalter High's 'Most Successful Son'. Could be a motive for murder. What's the name of his foreman. Get him on the phone.

SERGEANT RILEY:

Right away sir. (Rings up Chadwick's foreman in Coweta County.) It's ringing, Sir. (Hands the phone to Lt. Dan.)

LT. DAN:

Thanks. Lieutenant Dan Yeager calling from Fitzwalter, Georgia. We're investigating the murder of Emily Wilson. We'd like to ask you a few questions, Sir. How long have you worked for her husband, Chadwick Wilson? (Pause.) You're recently hired? Who was the supervisor before you? (Pause.) I see. Can you give me his name and where I might reach him? (Pause. Lt. Dan writes down information and hands it to Sergeant Riley.) Thanks. Oh, by the way, do you know why this Frank Dudley left the company? (Pause.) No benefits ... a small operation ... borrowed from Pete to pay Paul. Thanks again. (Hangs up and turns to Sergeant Riley.)

LT. DAN: (CONT.)

Call the Carroll County Sheriff and tell them we need a cooperative effort to search the premises of Wilson's International Chemical Supply and to interview Frank Dudley. Interestingly enough, Frank Dudley's address places him as a neighbor of Chadwick's out in rural Carroll County.

SERGEANT RILEY:

I'm on it, Sir.

CUT TO: EXT./INT. LOCATION: Country home of Frank Dudley's adjacent to Chadwick's in Carroll County, GA. TIME: Late Saturday morning.

We see Lieutenant Dan and Sheriff McPherson, first on the porch, then inside the house of Frank Dudley where he resides with his family.

LT. DAN:

Lt. Dan: (Knocks on door. Lt. Dan is accompanied by Lt. Thomas McPherson, detective working for Carroll County. Frank Dudley answers door.)

Hi, I'm Lt. Dan Yeager from the Fitzwalter Police Department. This is Sheriff McPherson, Carroll County. We'd like to ask you a few questions concerning an on-going investigation of the homicide of Emily Wilson.

FRANK DUDLEY:

Yes, sure, come on in. (Officers enter the home and take a seat.) I've been following it on the news. What a shame. Ms. Emily was a really nice lady. Can I get you something to drink. (Calls back to wife in kitchen.) Mother, put some coffee on.

LT. DAN:

No, no thanks. We just had breakfast.

FRANK DUDLEY:

Sure? Never mind, Mother. (A couple of children peek around the kitchen door.) You kids, go on out and play now. Ya here? (Directs conversation to his wife.) Take the kids out for a while, Dear. Thanks. (We hear indistinct chattering and door shutting as his wife steps outside with children by the back door. Dudley turns his attention back to the officers.)

LT. DAN:

I see you are neighbors with Chadwick Wilson, the decease's husband and it is our understanding you are his former employee. How many years have you known Chadwick?

FRANK DUDLEY:

You mean, Chad? I responded to an ad in the local paper about eight years ago ... about the same time when me and the wife watched him move in. Funny, Chad was my boss and also my neighbor. Couldn't believe anybody would buy that old rundown shack, though it did come with thirty acres and a chicken house. Worth fixing up, but I don't see where he did much fixin' ... maybe the front steps that fell through on him when he was proudly surveying his new acquisition. (Chuckles.) According to Chad, he didn't have a dime to his name when he bought the place. The bank lent him money for the farm and his new business, really, based on his Harvard degree. It was his plan to have Emily get up at dawn and cull out the dead chicks from the broods in the chicken house.

LT. DAN:

And she went along with that?

LT. MCPHERSON:

Didn't have to. No reputable poultry company would do business with him after he was found in violation of Code 3704. He was cited for failing to haul off household garbage and old tires which were accumulating in his barn. He was ordered to clean it up. It took him several truck loads to haul it off to the county dump. (Lt. Dan takes notes.)

FRANK DUDLEY:

Yes, the man always was skirting the law. Had a streak of rebellion towards authority which seemed to impress the company of vagrants and unsavory characters that hung around him.

LT. MCPHERSON:

Was he creating health hazards at the company. Is this why you left? Were there safety violations?

FRANK DUDLEY:

Not really. He didn't want trouble with his business. But I didn't appreciate him bringing some of those questionable characters near my family. He had this young, mentally challenged adult, Lennie, one of his employees, living in a converted shed in his backyard. The kid wasn't the problem ... but his family. (Shakes his head.) His mother, Bonnie Crabbs, had a string of husbands who were in the habit of dying mysteriously of similar gastric symptoms and her brother, Dewey ... well, I wouldn't put anything past him.

SHERIFF MCPERSON:

Carroll County's familiar with her brother, Dewey ... solid alibi ... He's in prison for assault with a deadly weapon.

LT. DAN:

(Turns to Sheriff McPherson.) I'd check out this Bonnie Crabbs. Our murderer's profile has all the earmarks of a woman's touch ... poison ... weapon of choice. (Turns to Frank Dudley.) Can you cast any more light on the unscrupulous qualifications of Chadwick's associates?

FRANK DUDLEY:

The truth be told, I believe he surrounded himself with people he could easily manipulate like Lennie. 'My way, or the highway,' was his favorite saying. Don't think he bargained for Bonnie Crabbs.

LT. DAN:

What's with the smelly garbage deal?

FRANK DUDLEY:

He's a big talker. Had a lot of stories to entertain with. Hey, now that I'm thinking about it, I do remember him telling a story about a woman driven insane by her husband by odiferous means. There was an incident that he said occurred when he was in college in Georgia. His Psychology 101 class took a field trip to a mental institute in Midville. This older lady, one of the inmates, runs up to him and gives him a big hug. He slowly recognizes her as Ms. Hattie, the former librarian from Fitzwalter. It was like an ole' fashion homecoming;

but it was, uh ... you know ... at the funny farm. Said he was shocked and embarrassed to see her. Referred to Ms. Hattie as a "cultural bum".

LT. DAN:

Everyone in Fitzwalter knew about Mad Hattie, former librarian turned bag lady. Her husband had had her sent up to Midville. "Cultural bum" ... interesting.(Makes note.)

LT. MCPHERSON:

Why was she institutionalized?

FRANK DUDLEY:

Apparently, humiliation. Shortly after they married, her husband began to change. He wasn't much for bathing or shaving. Wore the same old overalls and kept her in rags too. He made sure she couldn't get to her job on time, which resulted in her being fired. Then he gave her the responsibility of slopping the hogs. Nobody would go near the place or her because of the stench. Later she was seen around town pushing an old cart full of books and quoting Shakespeare.

LT. DAN:

Um ... I'm beginning to see what someone meant when they said he was full of copy-cat ideas ... just follow his stories. What else can you tell us about ... Chad's relationship with his wife?

FRANK DUDLEY:

They were separated you know. His decision, not her's. Chad would quote, 'It is better to live in an attic alone than in a house with a quarrelsome wife'... What he meant to say was, 'It is better to live apart with your mistress than in a house with a jealous wife'.

LT. DAN:

Yes, he did mention he was living at his office. I take it you liked Ms. Emily.

FRANK DUDLEY:

She was a sweet lady. (Looks down and shakes his head.) I tried to warn her. He was paying more-and-more attention to someone on his computer at the expense of his business. Irate suppliers would call in to complain about late payments. He wasn't getting the orders out on time either.

LT. DAN:

To whom was he communicating via the computer for long periods of time ... as you say?

FRANK DUDLEY:

I don't know, Sir. All I know is, he was allocating more of the day-to-day responsibilities to me ... with no extra pay or any benefits. So, I quit.

LT. DAN:

Is there anything else you'd like to share?

FRANK DUDLEY:

Yes, he had Howard Hughes' eccentricities without his billions.

LT. DAN:

What do you mean?

FRANK DUDLEY:

Had to have two of everything ... I mean he had a generator-backup for his generator. In his office, which wasn't very large to begin with, he had two compact refrigerators, two burner stoves, two hot water heaters ....

LT. DAN:

Two women, to state the obvious. (Turns to Sheriff McPherson.) Will be needing a subpoena for his computers.

LT. MCPHERSON:

We're already on it.

LT. DAN:

Did this same personality quirk manifest itself in his house in Carroll Country?

FRANK DUDLEY:

No, and oddly enough that's where it was needed.

LT. DAN:

What do you mean?

FRANK DUDLEY:

At least once a year, without fail, I'd see Chad leaning over that old well pump trying to get water to the pipes. He never would allow Emily to call a plumber ... said he might overcharge. Well, one winter when he got back from an out-of-town business trip, he had a good laugh around the office describing his wife's appearance ... hair plastered down to her head from not being able to wash for a week. He thought it was a hoot.

LT. DAN:

Sounds like something he would find amusing. How'd she take it?

FRANK DUDLEY:

She was humiliated at work. Seems her coworkers went to the principal complaining of her lack of personal hygiene. Chad told her they were just jealous of her being married to a Harvard man and all that. Ironic, un?

LT. DAN:

Right, ironic.

CUT TO: INT. LOCATION: LT. DAN'S OFFICE IN FITZWALTER TIME: MIDDAY

Lt. Dan and Sergeant Riley are studying the "Evidence Board". A picture of Chadwick Wilson is pinned to the board with two attached strings, one attached to a picture of Sheila Turner and the other attached to a picture of Bonnie Crabbs. A picture of Dave Richards stands alone.

LT. DAN:

Well, we can eliminate Bonnie Crabbs. McPherson just called. Said she has an airtight alibi.

SERGEANT RILEY:

Let me guess. She was either getting married or having a funeral.

LT.DAN

The former.

SERGEANT RILEY:

Who would marry her and why does she get away with her spouses' suspicious deaths?

LT. DAN:

Bad girls have their own allure ... otherwise known as a death wish. Her husbands were drunks and long estranged from their families. Quick cremations and no complaints. However, the insurance companies are investigating. They notified all local funeral homes not to do anymore cremations until they have a chance for their coroner to do an autopsy on any request from Bonnie Crabbs.

SERGEANT RILEY:

Then what was the connection between her and Chadwick? Was she possibly hired to kill Emily? We checked his bank statements and didn't find any out-of-the-ordinary transactions around the time of the reunion.

LT. DAN:

Like Dudley said, Chadwick surrounded himself with disreputable people, but I think he was out of his league with this crowd. The Crabbs are a criminal family. They're known throughout Georgia, Alabama, and Florida's penal system. They stick up for each other and do each other's bidding.

SERGEANT RILEY:

What besides being the mother of one of his employees would cause their paths to cross?

LT. DAN:

Get me Katrina Sommers on the phone. Maybe she can fill in the blanks.

SERGEANT RILEY:

Yes, Sir. (Riley looks up the number, calls Katrina, and hands phone to Lt. Dan.)

LT. DAN:

Hi Lieutenant Dan. How are you? Good, thanks. Hope I've caught you at a convenient time. I want to thank you again for all your help. Do you mind answering a few more questions concerning the case.

KATRINA:

No, not at all. Please, I miss Emilia every day. Anything I can do to help.

LT. DAN:

Did you know about the Crabbs ... Lennie and more specifically, his mother, Bonnie Crabbs?

KATRINA:

She was hired to care for Emilia after her episode in the hospital. That was a couple of years back. She just happened to be his employee's mother, a matter of convenience. Lennie was living on their farm at the time. Emelia told me she saw this Crabbs woman giving Chadwick the eye. Chadwick said he didn't trust her. When he didn't respond to her advances, she brought over Lennie's underaged teen sister. I'm sure he had better sense than to fall for the obvious bait. That's all I know about them. Emilia got better and all the Crabbs left.

LT. DAN:

Thanks again. Call if you think of anything else.

KATRINA:

Sure, whatever I can do. Glad to help. Bye for now.

LT. DAN:

Chadwick was scared of Bonnie Crabbs. Said she gave him the willies.

SERGEANT RILEY:

I'd be scared of Bonnie Crabbs too.

LT. DAN:

The truth be told, Chadwick may have flirted with doing harm to his wife, but he wasn't one hundred percent sure Granny was wrong. Granny had approved of Emily. He had a divided mind.

SERGEANT RILEY:

Katrina Sommers thinks he is capable of murder.

LT. DAN:

An opportunist, maybe. But he likes to be in control. I'm sure he realized he couldn't manipulate a manipulator like Bonnie Crabbs, a rougher hewn version of Sheila. And flaunting her daughter in front of him ... he had better sense than that ... especially on the heels of that police interrogation at the ER. He clearly passed up that opportunity to use the expertise of Bonnie Crabbs. We're looking for someone with more finesse. Someone that reminded him of his youth.

SERGEANT RILEY:

A midlife crisis?

LT. DAN:

Could be. Who knows what was in his head? Was he still trying to prove Granny Rutler wrong for interfering with his relationship with Sheila?

SERGEANT RILEY:

But Granny Rutler is long since dead.

LT. DAN:

Doesn't matter. He definitely resented being told who he could or could not marry.

SERGEANT RILEY:

Well Lieutenant, if we stick to our theory that the crime was committed by a woman, that leaves Sheila Turner. Where's the blurred line that she won't cross?

LT. DAN:

I'm not totally ruling out Dave Richards. Remember he is in the landscaping profession and would have easy access to oleander. He works for the county, and they have miles of scenic roads lined with this exotic toxic. He definitely bears more scrutiny.

SERGEANT RILEY:

Yea, but where's the motive? What did Emily Wilson ever do to him?

LT. DAN:

He and Chadwick are longtime rivals.

SERGEANT RILEY:

Yea, in wrestling tournaments.

LT. DAN:

He probably surmised that Chadwick wasn't quite deserving of all the accolades being bestowed on him. Possibly he wondered about the same things we did. Eyebrows must have been raised when the Wilsons arrived in that rattling, exhaust-billowing, old van. Or perhaps Emily inadvertently said something about how tight money was. She was still wearing that same old dress. Just perhaps, now bear with me, this is just a theory ... he threatened to expose Chadwick as a sham, a less-than-successful, hyped-up businessman.

SERGEANT RILEY:

Blackmail. But why kill her?

LT. DAN:

He wanted her in on it. She wouldn't go along with the plot and would have denied any accusations against Chadwick. According to Katrina, Emily was blindly loyal to her husband and would have come to his defense. She believed in marriage and wanted to save hers.

SERGEAT RILEY:

So, at that point, her life became the threat to motivate the payoff.

LT. DAN:

Little did Dave realize Chadwick's propensity for putting Emily at risk ... that or ... Chadwick didn't take Dave seriously because he was confident in his success and was just hiding his wealth from Emily. Wouldn't be the first husband to hide assets from his wife especially if he wanted a divorce.

SERGEANT RILEY:

No offense, Sir, but extortion? That does sound a little farfetched.

LT. DAN:

How so?

SERGEANT RILEY:

Interesting theory, but there's one glaring problem ... no evidence. And why didn't Chadwick say anything if he was being blackmailed?

LT. DAN:

Maybe he told Dave to go ahead with whatever. He wasn't about to get any money from him. After Emily's murder, he certainly didn't want those remarks coming out. He only insinuated something nefarious about Dave dancing with Emily. Of course, he would claim no knowledge of blackmail.

SERGEANT RILEY:

But Dave would never admit to extortion, so what would Chadwick say was the motive?

LT. DAN:

Jealousy. They were rivals. Because Chadwick was the husband, he thought he could set him up as the most likely suspect. And even if evidence of a blackmail attempt came out, not succumbing to blackmail is not a crime. Chadwick would ostensibly get away with murder by proxy.

SERGEANT RILEY:

And his hands would be clean.

LT. DAN:

Get Dave Richards on the phone and set up another interview ... a sober interview this time.

SERGEANT RILEY:

Sure, right away. (Sergeant Riley gets no response on the phone and leaves a message.) Hope he's not out on a drunk.

LT. DAN:

Go by his place of work. I want him in my office sometime today.

SERGEANT RILEY:

A warrant, sir?

LT. DAN:

Not yet. Let's see how cooperative he is. Don't really have any evidence linking him to the case other than proximity to the victim at the night of the event. Let me know as soon as he's located. I'm going home to eat lunch.

CUT TO: INT. LOCATION: Lt. DAN AND HAZEL'S KITCHEN/ DINING AREA TIME: NOON

We see Hazel preparing lunch and talking as she is walking back and forth to the dining table serving food. Lt. Dan is seated. Later Hazel sits down and continues the conversation with him as they have lunch.

HAZEL:

So, how are things going with the Wilson case?

LT. DAN:

We've ruled out Bonnie Crabbs ... firm alibi, but have not ruled out anyone linked to her ... Why Chadwick surrounds himself with questionable people is mind boggling. Looking in another direction now ... to one who was paying an inordinate amount of attention to Emily that night.

HAZEL:

You mean Dave Richards? They certainly were the center of attention while they were dancing ... a regular Patrick Swayze and Jennifer Grey. But dancing together doesn't mean ...

LT. DAN:

(Interrupts Hazel.) Dave Richards. He has access to and knowledge of oleander. Just don't know how I'm going to prove it. Still waiting on forensics to come up with something.

HAZEL:

What about the computers confiscated from Chadwick's office? Have the emails been retrieved? They ought to answer a lot of questions.

LT. DAN:

Our tech team is still working on them. All in good time. No stone left aright.

HAZEL:

Seems to me the elephant in the room is named Sheila. I still say there's something bizarre about her getting married every five years exactly after the reunions.

LT. DAN:

Maybe it's her way of reliving her glory days ... She was a very popular girl. Maybe she's out to prove she still is.

HAZEL:

She changes husbands quinquennially ... same time, same venue ... just like clockwork. Who does that?

LT. DAN:

You're making too much of happenstance.

HAZEL:

She's either rebounding from being rebuffed by someone or she's trying to manipulate someone by making them jealous. No one falls in love on cue. Either way it gives Scuttlebutt Bertha plenty to talk about. (Phone rings and Lt. Dan answers it.)

LT. DAN:

What do you mean, 'He didn't show up for work'? (pause) He's taking Dave Jr. to rehab. Why? What happened with his son? (pause) Again, ok, the Serenity Hill Rehab in Coffee County. Got it. (Turns to Hazel) See you later. Got to run.

HAZEL:

Bye, Honey. (They kiss goodbye.)

CUT TO: INT. LOCATION: SERENITY HILLS REHABILITATION CENTER TIME: MID MORNING

WE see Dave Richards helping his son fill out admission forms in the lobby of the rehab center. They give them to the receptionist. Lt. Dan enters just as they finish up and Dave Jr.'s name is called. He leaves with the nurse after father and son hug.

LT. DAN:

I'm sorry to hear about your son's drug bust ... His second, I believe, this year.

DAVE RICHARDS:

I know you're thinking, like father ... like son, but it's not like that. This is Sheila's carnage. She's the one who emotionally abandoned our son for her precious Chadwick. She said she wasn't going to let anyone stand in her way. She was furious with Chadwick for not standing up to Granny who put the total blame of her alleged pregnancy on her, calling her every derogatory name in the book. Granny disgraced her throughout Fitzwalter and most importantly in her father's eyes.

LT. DAN:

You're referring to Mr. Harris. It is my understanding Mr. Harris wanted Chadwick to come into his vending machine business.

DAVE RICHARDS:

Mr. Harris had treated Chadwick like an honored guest in their home. He couldn't believe he brought embarrassment to his family. He already had a history of heart disease and the stress proved too much. His death in the wake of Granny's vile attacks sent Sheila over the edge.

LT. DAN:

Over the edge ... So, you're saying to redeem her self-esteem and justify her father's death, Sheila elevated their puppy love into a religious quest ... a life pursuit, that would cost any and all who got in her way like, for instance ... Emily. Am I reading you correctly?

DAVE RICHARDS:

You got it. She's bonkers. She said she married me to get back at Chadwick and he made matters worse by making our child the excuse as to why they couldn't be together ... and later his own son. He in essence was dangling her along. Maybe she decided to call his bluff and expedite the situation.

LT. DAN:

What about her marriages to Blake and Turner?

DAVE RICHARDS:

Same reason she married me. On the heels of being put off by Chadwick again and again. I would say they were marriages to push-Chadwick's-buttons. Sheila is very manipulative. She'll use anyone to get what she wants. She's made an example for Chadwick to follow on how-to-divorce-your-spouse. I hope they do get married and get a good dose of each other. If it weren't for their double-suicide, even Romeo and Juliette's rose-colored glasses would have fogged over in time. A little of, 'Honey, don't forget to take out the garbage,' has a way of bringing lovebirds back to reality.

LT. DAN:

How did you know about Chadwick's reluctance to take out the garbage?

DAVE RICHARDS:

Just speaking figuratively. I don't wish them to get married enough to get Emily out of the way. Maybe Sheila would. She's the crazy one. Believe me, she'd do anything to marry Chadwick.

LT. DAN:

Or maybe, you were trying to topple Chadwick off his pedestal and tried to get Emily to admit he was a failure. According to Emily's best friend and confidant, Katrina Sommers, they lived a rags-to-rags existence, but Emily wouldn't have gone along with that description ... she could see no wrong in Chadwick. If he said money was being invested in the business, she totally accepted that.

DAVE RICHARDS:

I have no idea what you're talking about.

LT. DAN:

You surmised Emily to be very naive. You figured he must have money hidden somewhere, so you attempted to blackmail him by threatening to end Emily's life who, despite Sheila's ploys, he continued to stay married to.

DAVE RICHARDS:

What proof of blackmail do you have? (Lt. Dan makes no response.) I thought so. That's because there was no blackmail.

LT. DAN:

You were the last one seen in the company of Emily, and you were seen plying her with alcohol.

DAVE RICHARDS:

If I were going to murder someone, I would have murdered Sheila a long time ago. And as for Emily, she nursed that one drink during the whole of our conversation.

LT. DAN:

A conversation concerning what?

DAVE RICHARDS:

I felt sorry for Emily, that's all. She was clueless. She talked a little about her school days and how she was shy and instinctively stayed away from teenage cliques. She likened them to William Golding's "Lord of the Flies" ... children sans civilization. But said she was enjoying the reunion because it was like going to the prom with mature adults ... respectable members of the community. She couldn't conceive of the idea of anyone there being bent on doing-her-in.

LT. DAN:

Where did the bail money come from ... $50,000. on top of rehab? Who's paying Dave Jr.'s bills?

DAVE RICHARDS:

Sheila ... she's the cause of his problems and he's giving problems back to her. She's going broke ... another reason she's desperate to marry Chadwick. She's taken out loans on her house to pay for the bail money and other accrued debt.

LT. DAN:

You work a lot with oleander in your landscape work, right?

DAVE RICHARDS:

Sure. Why?

LT. DAN:

You realize it's quite poisonous.

DAVE RICHARDS:

It's a popular shrub, Lieutenant. Also fast growing and easily propagated. Almost everyone has them in their yard including Sheila's. So what?

LT. DAN:

(Looks reflective.) You're sure Emily only had one drink?

DAVE RICHARDS:

Certain. If she was drunk, it wasn't self-induced.

LT. DAN:

Ok, sorry to have bothered you. Wish you and your son well. Just doing my job. You understand. (Lt. Dan leaves and makes a phone call to Hazel.)

LT. DAN: (ON THE PHONE TO HAZEL)

Hi Honey. Meet me down at the precinct at two o'clock. (Pause) I'd like a woman's perspective on something. (Pause) Yes, that's what I said. Ok, see you there.

CUT TO: INT. LOCATION: POLICE PRECINCT TIME: TWO O'CLOCK.

We see a meeting of Sergeant Riley's class of rookie police officers seated facing a man from forensics and a computer specialist. Sergeant Riley standing by the door, gives a slight look of surprise when he sees Hazel walk in with Lt. Dan.

LT. DAN:

Gentlemen, you know my wife, Mrs. Yeager. (Men nod their heads looking a little bewildered.) Never hurts to get a woman's insight. One of our main suspects presently is a woman, Sheila ... in a long-standing love/hate relationship with our victim's husband. We'll be looking for any evidence that might link her to the crime while of course keeping an open mind and not ruling out other possibilities.

HAZEL:

(Hazel stares in wonderment at Lt. Dan.) What did Dave say in that interview to switch your focus back on a female?

LT. DAN:

I haven't totally switched my focus.

ROOKIE I:

(Raises hand.) What about Dave Richards? He was the last one seen with the victim on the night of the reunion.

LT. DAN:

He's a possibility. Maybe a blackmail attempt gone wrong. He partly blames Chadwick for causing resentment between Sheila and Dave Jr. Thinks he's been dangling Sheila along for years. His son in particular is having drug abuse problems.

ROOKIE I:

I thought Dave Sr. was the addict. An addiction to drugs might be genetic. Maybe he passed it to his son.

LT. DAN:

A tendency to abuse chemicals might be genetic. But Dave's problems with alcohol started after the divorce and were not the cause of the divorce according to his parents, the main caregivers to Dave Jr. Dave Sr. blamed Chadwick for a lot of his problems. I'm not totally ruling him out. We'll see where the evidence takes us.

ROOKIE II:

Most murdered women are done-in by their intimate partners. That would point the finger at Chadwick Wilson.

LT. DAN:

Yes, Chadwick is still very much on our radar. But he would have had to have had an accomplice as he was in constant view of the other guests at the event.

ROOKIE II:

A female accomplice?

LT. DAN:

Most likely, but not Bonnie Crabbs. She'd more likely to have made him the victim. (Low snickering among rookies.) If there are no more questions, we'll turn it over to Reginald, our computer tech expert. (Turns to Reginald.) So, who is Chadwick's mystery woman?

REGINALD:

Someone calling themselves, Scuttlebutt Bertha. Over 500 emails between them leading up to the murder.

EVERYONE COLLECTIVELY:

(Look of surprise as they shake their heads in disbelief.) Scuttlebutt Bertha?

LT.DAN:

Hardly seems like his type. What were they communicating about?

REGINALD:

Recipes. Seems she's a cook, you know ... cook for the Fitzwalter High School ... but beyond that ... they're talking gourmet cooking. I'd say they're passionate about swapping gourmet recipes.

LT. DAN:

Excuse me. Did I hear you right? Was there some kind of secret code being passed between the salmon fritters and the crepe suzettes?

REGINALD:

Food peppered with a lot of spicy gossip. I'd say, particularly, gossip about Sheila Turner and the unhappy state of her present marriage and, likewise, Chadwick Wilson grumbling about the unhappy state of his marriage.

LT. DAN:

Now we're getting to it. So, Chadwick was complaining about Emily. What about?

REGINALD:

Something about her being a "cultural bum" always "thinking". Said he made her 'tote the water and cut the firewood' sort of speak. Asked her, 'What do you "think" about that'. They both had laughs at Emily's expense.

LT. DAN:

Class warfare.

REGINALD:

Actually, he seemed more interested in the conversations about food.

LT. DAN:

Food?

REGINALD:

If anything, he complained about Emily's obsession with wanting him to diet. This man loves food. If he related any story about any places that he visited or adventures he went on ... it was usually centered on where he dined and what was served. He reminisces in great detail about delicious culinary dishes: the appetizers, main entrees, side dishes that he enjoyed decades ago with great relish. No pun intended.

LT. DAN:

Conspiracies, conspiracies. Get to it. Besides gastronomic delights, what if anything salacious was going on. What evidence did you get out of these emails? What was his motive for moving out of his home into his office?

REGINALD:

I don't know. He repeated several times that he and Emily were separated. That he had told her unequivocally he was leaving her after their son graduated from high school. He wanted his son to get a degree in business from his college and join him in his company. Said his son had other ideas, but that wasn't important to him. He knew what was best for his son.

LT. DAN:

Same controlling behavior evidenced in all his relationships.

REGINALD:

Strange, because he then related a story about one of his college classmates who had fallen out with his father due to the same controlling attitude. His father had mapped out his son's life, but it became obvious his son was going in another direction.

LT. DAN:

Raising someone doesn't guarantee loyalty or even gratitude. Same goes for marriage. What else was in the emails? I'm not seeing a murder conspiracy here.

REGINALS:

There was a great deal of talk about arrangements for the reunion. Scuttlebutt Bertha was talking excessively about expectations of a large turnout. There would be live entertainment, raffles, dining, and dancing … everything first class.

HAZEL:

If it weren't for Scuttlebutt Bertha, the-go-between, there wouldn't have been any reconnection between Chadwick and Sheila. There great romance was being stoked by the fires of that main-events hostess as surely if she were flambéing cherries jubilee. As the organizer of the 95th Reunion she was setting the stage for a Broadway production … Fitzwalter's own Romeo and Juliette.

LT. DAN:

I'm not so sure who was directing whom. Neither the emails nor their phones show any direct collaboration between Chadwick and Sheila. If she was his accomplice, they had to have been sending messages through Scuttlebutt Bertha, and we just don't see the subterfuge in the succotash. However, there is something uncanny going on with his stories.

REGINALD:

He did mention seeing the movie "White Oleander" starring Michelle Pfeiffer.

LT. DAN:

Well, that would be laughable in court. What have you got for hard evidence, Henry? Henry, from Forensics … Henry stand up. (Henry stands up.) Did you find any prints on the empty bottle of Wild Turkey found near the victim's body?

HENRY:

No, it was wiped clean … not even her lipstick was on the rim.

LT. DAN:

Well, what about the trash bags? Anything of interest there?

HENRY:

Mostly food and paper products ... some disposable culinary ware including plastic gloves, utensils, a turkey baster.

LT. DAN:

A disposable turkey baster?

HAZEL:

They did serve hors d'oeuvres with turkey, as I recall.

SERGEANT RILEY:

We were able to procure many photos and videos from that night, Sir. However, we've been over and over the pictures and have been unable to find one single picture showing anyone pinning the poisonous corsage on the victim. (Points to projected picture.) We see here the arrival of Chadwick and Emily to the dance. You will notice the victim is already wearing the oleander corsage as she arrives. The other female attendees received their freesia corsages at the gymnasium.

LT. DAN:

Earlier in the day, the class dined at the banquet hall of the Yankee-Dixie Townhouse Restaurant and Inn.

SERGEANT RILEY:

Right. We have video footage documenting the previous festivities at the banquet hall.

LT. DAN:

Show us what you have, Sergeant.

LT. DAN:

Bear with me as I backtrack to the noon hour. (He adjusts equipment.) You will note, people are wearing more casual attire here including Chadwick and Emily. (Pauses video.) You will also notice name cards indicating prearranged seating assignments. Emily and Chadwick Wilson are seated opposite Sheila.

LT. DAN:

Who made the arrangements?

HAZEL:

Scuttlebutt Bertha and the other female members on the committee.

SERGEANT RILEY:

Here you can see Miss Thompson at the head of the table welcoming the class and extolling their virtues, past and present. In particular she gives recognition to Chadwick Wilson for being the first alumnus to obtain a master's degree from Harvard University and subsequently starting his own business, Wilson International Chemicals, INC.

PAN TO VIDEO: INT. LOCATION: BANQUET ROOM OF YANKEE-DIXIE TOWNHOUSE RESTAURANT TIME: NOONDAY

We are viewing the video just as people are applauding Chadwick. Sheila is applauding too but is noticeably staring down at her green peas. Miss Thompson sits down, and Bertha takes the stand with a large raffle jar. Applause subsides.

BERTHA:

We are so grateful for our generous sponsors who have provided raffle gifts for our class reunion guests. We would especially like to thank the Okefenokee Swamp Wood Hope Chests Company. (She holds up a beautifully polished wooden jewelry box with one hand. With her other hand, she reaches into the raffle jar and pulls out a slip of paper. She appears to read.) Emily Wilson. Congratulations. You have won a beautiful cypress jewelry box, a miniature replica of an Okefenokee Swamp Wood Hope Chests.

EMILY:

I can't believe it. I never win anything.

(Emily walks up to the head table to receive her prize. Camera does close-up of jewelry box. Emily doesn't seem to notice that the design of the box looks more like a casket than a hope chest. It's an oblong box, 12"x6"x4", with a mounded top and inlaid trim. Six small brass handles, purely decorative, are symmetrically fastened around the edges. It apparently is a music box as it has a wind-up key on its side. Emily opens the box to show a beautiful oleander corsage wrapped in cellophane lying on a white silk-lined cushion. Immediately, it plays Chopin's "Funeral March".)

EMILY:

Oh, how beautiful ... I love Chopin's Sonata #2. It's my favorite. I'll be sure and wear the corsage tonight at the dance. (Emily takes her seat.)

COLLECTIVE AUDIENCE:

(Everyone's eyes are riveted to Emily as if they are witnessing a sacrificial ritual. Slowly becoming aware of their own prolonged stares, they follow Bertha's lead and begin applauding.)

ACT III

PAN BACK TO: INT, LOCATION: POLICE PRECINT TIME: SAME DAY
CONT.

We see everyone in the room: Lt. Dan, Sergeant Riley, Reginald, Henry, Hazel,
and the Rookie Policemen also in stunned silence.

LT.DAN:
(Look of disbelief on face. Finally breaks silence in room.) Well, I think we can
safely rule out Dave Richards.

ROOKIE II:
(Raises hand and is recognized.) Bertha Quick is a cook. One would think her
method of killing would be through food.

LT. DAN:
Too obvious. No, that would have readily indicated her. Richards was being
set-up as the fall guy. Had to be something linked to him ... landscaping and/or
alcohol. She was probably hoping to pass it off as an accidental case of too much
drinking. But no one has testified that Emily was ever a heavy drinker. This
includes her husband which appears to give him "clean hands".

ROOKIE I:
So, how did the Wild Turkey get into her system?

LT. DAN:
Ole Scuttlebutt has a sense of humor ... the turkey baster, of course ... gavage,
better known as forced feeding. It's the way the French make foie gras, by
ramming feed down the throats of ducks or geese to fatten up their livers. It's
considered a delicacy. Once Emily had passed out from the oleander, Bertha
administered the Wild Turkey. (Turns to Henry.) What about the turkey
baster ... any prints?

HENRY:
Wiped clean. Some white gloves were found in the same proximity, however. You
want them swiped for DNA?

LT. DAN:
Yes, though that will take more time. Go ahead Riley, gather all the photos of
ladies wearing white gloves.

HAZEL:
I can tell you which ones were wearing white gloves ... all Scuttlebutt's planning
committee ... greeters, decorators, computer personnel in charge of invitations.
That would rule out Sheila. She's too arrogant to serve.

LT. DAN:

But not too arrogant for practicing cheers blocking the entrance to the ladies' locker room.

HAZEL:

You're right ... about 11:30, the cheerleaders were creating quite a distraction.

LT. DAN:

And simultaneously creating an alibi for Sheila.

SERGEANT RILEY:

This is all circumstantial evidence. There are no prints and no photos directly linking anyone to the crime. And for all we know, Emily pricked herself with the oleander corsage. Oleander is toxic but, in order to kill, it needs to enter the body, either by ingestion, injection, or breathing it in.

LT. DAN:

Like carbon monoxide. Ronnie Blake ... that's it. That was one conveniently timed suicide ... right around the third Class Reunion. Get Doc Cole on the phone.

CUT TO: INT. LOCATION: MORGUE TIME: AFTERNOON

We see Doc Cole stopping work on a corpse and cleaning up while talking to Lt. Dan.

LT. DAN:

The Ronnie Blake suicide. Did you do a test for toxicity?

DOC COLE:

No need to. Carbon monoxide was the obvious toxicant.

LT. DAN:

I have reason to believe Mr. Blake's suicide was staged ... something my wife, Hazel, said about the strange timing of his death right around the time of the Class of 95's third reunion in 2010.

DOC COLE:

The Class Reunion? Are we looking for oleander?

LT. DAN:

Possibly.

DOC COLE:

That was five years ago. If you're talking about finding traces after exhumation now, it could be a hit or a miss. Depends on conditions.

LT. DAN:

If nothing else, the dig will make certain parties nervous and ... nervous hands spill beans.

DOC COLE:

Blake was found in his truck in a closed-in garage. To stage it, and I'm assuming you're talking about his wife, Sheila, she would have had to place a 185 lb. man in the cab. If he was in an unconscious state, how could she have moved him from the house to the truck?

LT. DAN:

An accomplice ... Bertha Quick.

DOC COLE:

The cook at the high school? Why would she have a dog in that race?

LT. DAN:

I'm not sure. I do know she handed the murder weapon to Emily Wilson in a jewelry box given as a lottery prize at the reunion banquet.

DOC COLE:

The oleander corsage? Who pinned it on her?

LT. DAN:

We don't know. Possibly Chadwick, but I find it hard to believe he knowingly committed murder. I grew up with Chadwick. He likes mind games. Putting his wife in danger would be as far as he would go. Come to think of it ... involving her in a love triangle with a mentally unstable woman would be the ultimate danger zone.

CUT TO: EXT. LOCATION: FITZWALTER CEMETERY TIME: EARLY MORNING

We see Andy Flint from Atlanta On-The-Spot News reporting in a hushed, respectful voice as the body of Ronnie Blake is being exhumed. The police and a few Blake family members watch the disinterment proceedings.

ANDY FLINT:

Dave Richards is no longer a person of interest in the Emily Wilson case. Bertha Quick is now a suspect and is being held at the Fitzwalter Police Precinct.

(On-The-Spot News shows a video of Bertha Quick being arrested at the Fitzwalter High School. She is waving at the camera.)

ANDY FLINT:

The Georgia Department of Toxicology has confirmed that an oleander corsage given to the victim in a presumedly rigged door prize by the events coordinator, Bertha Quick, was the contributing cause of death. We have been told by the Fitzwalter authorities that it is believed that Quick, the alleged murderer, was not working alone, nor was this her first criminal involvement. Due to the suspicious timing of another death occurring around a previous Class of 95's reunions, our Fitzwalter coroner, Doc Cole, has changed Ronnie Blake's cause of death back in 2000 from suicide to inconclusive. His body is being disinterred for autopsy. We are watching the exhumation now. We will keep you informed of developments.

CUT TO: INT> LOCATION: SHEILA'S HOME TIME: MORNING

We see Sheila being arrested by Lt. Dan. Sergeant Riley is placing cuffs on her.

LT. DAN:

You are under arrest on suspicion of murder of your former husband, Ronnie Blake, who died of carbon monoxide poisoning on June 24, 2010, and on suspicion of being involved with the murder of Emily Wilson on June 15, 2015. You have the right to retain a lawyer. You have the right to remain silent. Anything you say can and will be used against you in a court of law.

SHEILA:

I'm innocent. You're making a mistake. Ronnie was sick. He was depressed because he had a terminal illness. He was taking a lot of experimental drugs at the time of his death.

LT. DAN:

There were enough drugs to kill a rat that managed to gnaw its way into the coffin.

SHEILA:

Prescription drugs. I had nothing to do with it. I was over at Bertha Quick's. Ask her.

LT. DAN:

We did. She's under arrest too. She's our main suspect. We believe the two of you were working together. She's presently in a holding cell down at the precinct.

SHEILA:

Nobody stages their husband's suicide. Everybody knows life insurance companies don't pay off for a suicide.

LT. DAN:

His property was left to you. Perhaps you were motivated by something other than money. You made a mistake commiserating with a compulsive gossip like Scuttlebutt Bertha. She couldn't keep her mouth shut if her life ... that is, your life depended on it.

SHEILA:

I want a lawyer.

CUT TO: INT. LOCATION: LT. DAN'S OFFICE AT POLICE HEADQUARTERS TIME: LATE MORNING

We see Sergeant Riley and Lt. Dan talking strategy.

SERGEANT RILEY:

Sheila's lawyered up. Not getting a word out of her.

LT. DAN:

Put her in Interrogation Room I and have another policeman put Bertha in Interrogation Room II. Be sure they see each other passing in the hallway. (Watches in-time surveillance camera on Bertha Quick pacing back and forth in Interrogation Room II. Sheila's head is down on folded arms on table in Interrogation Room I. She looks up as her lawyer enters.) Handle this with care. We don't want any errors on our part. Has Bertha been informed of her rights?

SERGEANT RILEY:

Yes, but she seems quite eager to talk.

LT. DAN:

Can't help herself. Let's do our thing.

SERGEANT RILEY:

As always, Sir.

CUT TO: INT. LOCATION: INTERROGATION ROOM II TIME: LATE MORNING

SERGEANT RILEY:

Well, Bertha Quick, looks like your next reunion will be in prison with your colleague in crime, Sheila Turner. And believe me, she's not as loyal as you think. Face it ... she's not your friend. She was just using you to get back with Chadwick.

BERTHA:

She was using me? No, no, no, I was using her. She and Chadwick were my inventions, my headliners. I'm the one who directed and wrote this script. Check

64

it out on my social media page, "Grapevine". I have over 13.2 million followers. This 4th Reunion of the Class of 95 was the grandest, most talked about event since Reconstruction. I'm a direct descendant of Philias P. Fitzwalter, the founder of our amalgamated town. These little old-school folk, like Emily Wilson, need to step aside. They're no match for a digital savvy media influencer like Scuttlebutt Bertha.

LT. DAN:

(Turns to Sergeant Riley.) What is she talking about?

SERGEANT RILEY:

I don't know, sir.

LT. DAN:

So, you're not denying that you had a hand in killing Emily Wilson?

BERTHA:

That little fleeting fad. She didn't deserve one of Fitzwalter's finest. (Mockingly speaks with a southern accent.) 'Oh, I just l-o-o-ve Chopin's Funeral March.' Are you kidding me. Nobody's that naive.

LT. DAN:

People who don't have devious minds don't readily attribute evil thoughts to those that have a veneer of respectability. It never crossed her mind that she would encounter adolescent barbarianism amongst middle-aged pillars of the community. She at least expected them to respect her marriage and motherhood.

BERTHA:

Archaic thinking. The only important thing is to be remembered.

SERGEANT RILEY:

Yes, who can forget Lizzie Borden?

LT. DAN:

And the oleander corsage that was raffled-off in a jewelry box ... did Chadwick have anything to do with that?

BERTHA:

Beware of Fitzwalters bearing gifts ... All my ideas ... the oleander, the Wild Turkey being dispensed with the turkey baster.

FLASHBACK: INT. LOCATION: LADIES' LOCKERROOM TIME: NIGHT OF REUNION

We see Bertha forcing alcohol down Emily's throat with the turkey baster. Emily is passed out, lying prostrate on the locker room floor. Later Bertha tosses the turkey baster and gloves into the trash as she leaves out the back way.

CUT TO: INT> LOCATION: INTERROGATION ROOM II TIME: LATE MORNING

We see the continuation of Bertha's interrogation by Lt. Dan and Sergeant Riley.

LT. DAN:
Dave Richards said you nudged him to dance with Emily that night.

BERTHA:
Set-up by the Mambo. Dancers give the impression of being a romantic nexus though the reality is they're two people trying really hard not to step on each other's feet. They aren't thinking about romance; they are concentrating on the count.

FLASHBACK: INT. LOCATION: GYM TIME: NIGHT OF REUNION

We hear Mambo music. We see Bertha videoing Dave Richards dancing with Emily Wilson with the entire class circling around them. People are staring at them with raised eyebrows. It appears Dave is whispering something seductive in Emily's ear as he dips her gracefully backwards, but a close up reveals he is merely counting.

BERTHA:
Don't they make a lovely couple?

EVELYN:
An adulterous couple.

DAVE RICHARDS:
(Camera slowly pans into close up of couple who can be heard counting.) 2-3-4-feet together, 2-3-4-feet together, 2-3-4-feet together. M-m-m-mambo.

CUT TO: INT. LOCATION: INTERROGATION ROOM II TIME: LATE MORNING

We see continuation of interrogation of Bertha by Lt. Dan and Sergeant Riley.

LT. DAN:
But who actually pinned the corsage on Emily?

BERTHA:

Now that, I couldn't tell you. Just a touch of secret ingredient.

LT. DAN:

Are you sure you don't want a lawyer? The court can appoint you one, Pro Bono.

BERTHA:

Know way. This is my show.

LT. DAN:

(Turns to Sergeant Riley.) The Mambo dance with Dave Richards ... Did you get all this on the record?

SERGEANT RILEY:

(Rolls eyes.) Like I say, this is one for the Yearbook of the Class of '95.

CUT TO: INT. LOCATION: LT. DAN AND HAZEL'S HOME TIME: EVENING

We see Hazel and Lt. Dan relaxing in their home at the end of the day. Lt. Dan pauses his remote control on the tv. Hazel closes her book.

HAZEL:

So, how did the interviews go?

LT. DAN:

Unbelievable. We got a "confession" of murder, or rather a "bragging" of murder from Bertha. She implicated no one else.

HAZEL:

She said nothing about Sheila.

LT. DAN:

Not a thing. We had to let her go. Insufficient evidence.

HAZEL:

What about the autopsy?

LT. DAN:

Doc Cole did find traces of oleander, but Ronnie Blake had been prescribed oleander as part of his experimental therapy by his doctor. We have nothing tying Sheila to her late husband's death or Emily Wilson's.

HAZEL:

And Bertha?

LT. DAN:

Claims Ronnie Blake's death was a suicide. Only takes responsibility for the death of Emily.

HAZEL:

So, you're saying Bertha gave a full confession for the death of Chadwick's wife, exonerating him too?

LT. DAN:

Exactly. She was bragging about her prowess as an events planner ... How the buzz about Sheila and Chadwick brought in a record crowd and millions of likes on "Grapevine".

HAZEL:

"Grapevine", her social media app?

LT. DAN:

And if you can believe it, she claims she cleared the way for them to marry. She takes full credit for the murder of Emily Wilson. Says it's a murder that will go down in digital history.

HAZEL:

She didn't post the actual murder ... did she?

LT. DAN:

We're looking into the dark web. So far, we've found the banquet, the dance sequence, and the discovery of Emily's body. The main narrative seems to be the timing of Sheila's marriages and the dates of the reunion.

HAZEL:

I knew there was something weird going on.

LT. DAN:

Bertha said she was descended from Philias P. Fitzwalter, and I guess she wanted to be famous too. Quite frankly, she makes Bonnie Crabbs look sane ... but killing to be remembered? What's with that?

HAZEL:

The Greeks believed only those that etched their memories into the minds of men were deserving of the pagan realm of Hades ... the quiet, unpretentious types like Emily were doomed to walk around in eternal despair.

LT. DAN:

The irony is Emily won't soon be forgotten. Neither will Sheila and Chadwick along with Bertha. Social media has blurred the lines between reality and fantasy ... Fame has become the new road to salvation.

HAZEL:

Revisited ... not new. Bertha Quick was feeding off the attention she received from the "clique". What's harder to understand is the motive of the "clique", the not-so-innocent audience to her theatrics. With technology, gossipmongering has expanded. People, to whom high school was the high point of their lives, stagnated into a group hooked on the "Sheila and Chadwick Soap Opera". And with a click-and-a-scroll they participated in the murder of Emily Wilson as surely as did Bertha Quick. Without them ... there would be no Scuttlebutt Bertha; without Scuttlebutt Bertha ... there would be no crime.

LT. DAN:

We'll never know Sheila's or Chadwick's actual participation. I heard they are already planning their wedding as soon as her divorce comes through.

HAZEL:

Emily's body is not even in the ground. Did he buy her an engagement ring?

LT. DAN:

A big one, so I've heard.

HAZEL:

How many carats?

LT. DAN:

Two, of course.

Printed in the United States
by Baker & Taylor Publisher Services